The Leadership Management Series
For
Managers & Partners
In the 21st Century
(2nd Edition)

Vocabulary & Axioms for Professional Managers and Partners

Gregory N. Weismantel

This book is dedicated to the late
Major General Fred F. Marty, U.S. Army
Leader, Patriot, Confidant, and Friend

Vocabulary & Axioms for
Professional Managers and Partners

ISBN: 978-0-9910961-0-7
Contact Information:
Greg Weismantel
Epic Management Group
473 Dunham Rd, Ste. 208
St. Charles, Il 60174
630.587.9988 x22
Greg.weismantel@epicglobaltech.com

EPIC is a leading provider of Leadership Management Consulting services for all sized
businesses throughout the United States and Canada. Its assignment with leading companies
includes use of its proprietary Strategic and Leadership Management processes which allow
companies to implement 3-year strategic growth initiatives within the framework of their
own operational processes. EPIC also provides these services for privately owned family
businesses where succession planning is involved for the retiring owner of the company.
The Epic Management Process includes development mentor programs for First Line,
Middle, Executive and CEO/Managing Partner levels of companies and firms.
www.EpicGlobalTech.com

Introduction

Becoming a Professional Manager or Partner is not easy. Why? It requires the individual to become something that is not easy for most people. A professional manager or partner is not a "doer." A great manager or partner is a leader of people who requires skills that are foreign to many. It requires knowledge of situations and the ability to convince others to explore new ways of approaching old habits, and understanding the difference between responsibility and accountability.

Leadership management is the hardest of work whether you work in a firm or a company. Why, you ask? Because being an exceptional manager or partner requires exceptional leadership and implementing the art of leading people to achieve common goals. Specialist work is the easy work, and is regimented and rote, often making it boring. There will never be anything boring about the work of a Professional Manager or Partner because it requires an individual who can unify the specialists to accomplish common objectives through and with others, utilizing six functions of management: _Strategy, Planning, Organizing, Leadership, Teamwork, and Control._

The process of managing occurs in every company and partnership in the world. It happens in professional partnerships, in CPA firms, law firms, and physician groups as well as multi-national companies, and grocery stores. The sad reality is that the Grand Recession of 2008 forced many managers and partners back into being the best specialist, not the best manager, not the best partner. The time has come to reverse that trend and take action at becoming Professional Managers and Partners again.

To do so, one must master the functions, techniques and activities of managing people, and understanding accountability is the key.

This is a requirement of every enterprise from the president or managing partner to the floor leader. But there is logic involved that must be mastered by the young as well as the experienced manager.

The Epic Group of management consultants has executive management experience. We have been there and done that. We have helped develop managers and management processes in large and small companies and firms, such as Martin Marietta, Lockheed, Commonwealth Edison, Arthur Andersen, Asea Brown Boveri, Mueller LLC, Doran Scales, the Norix Group and others. Through our vast managerial experience we have recognized a pattern of management axioms and techniques that all successful companies use, and so we bring excitement to the mundane view of managing in a company or firm. We will identify the logic that is involved to make your job fun. The rest is up to you!

The first step is to communicate properly, utilizing a common vocabulary which everyone in your company or firm can comprehend. The clarity of meaning in communicating has everything to do with accomplishing the proper metric for success. In order to accomplish this I have devoted countless years in studying how successful CEOs, Presidents and Managing Partners manage properly, and they all begin by communicating with their executive direct reports and other managers within their companies and firms.

Through the years, that need prompted me to develop a common use of terms and words linked to axioms in management tenets which I have observed that all successful companies utilize.

This book is entitled _Vocabulary & Axioms for Professional Managers and Partners_ and is intended to be used by every manager and partner within a company and firm, so that we all have the same vocabulary and understanding in managing with accountability.

I urge you to read the definitions of management terms placed herein, along with the commentary which describes how each definition relates to the core process of management. An alphabetical list of definitions is provided on the page following the last word "Zilch," and then followed by some powerful Axioms in Management Tenets that complete the publication.

You will notice that the first word in the vocabulary is out of alphabetical order. The word is "Accountability," and always comes first in any manager or partner's core process of leadership management.

If at any time you need to discuss these definitions and axioms feel free to contact me at the phone or email address shown in the front of the book. I have mentored many great CEOs, Managers and Partners in my day, and you will probably fit in well with that group of professionals.

Gregory Weismantel

Gregory N. Weismantel
Epic Management Group

"…a man does not build a business, he builds an organization. The organization builds the business."

John D. Rockefeller

A

Accountability, Definition of

Is the combining of the responsibility, the fixed duties or work, along with the authority given by a higher level to complete the responsibility, and agreed to by the individual accepting the responsibility. *(See Accountability, Requirements for; Responsibility)*

It is important for a manager or partner to understand the difference between Responsibility and Accountability.

Accept

To agree to take upon oneself the duties or responsibilities which are offered from a higher level of authority.

In management terms, to accept or agree with the work and authority to complete the work is the third requirement for having accountability between levels of management.

Accepting

Compliance by an employee or member of a team with the objectives and metrics provided by an individual who has a higher level of authority so that accountability for the objectives and metrics is established between them.

A management process requires that employees and team members of lower levels of authority are linked with the objectives and metrics of higher levels of management so that the entire company is proceeding on the same mission of the company. Accepting the objective along with the metric is key to establishing accountability throughout the entire company or firm. (See Metric)

Accountability, Line

Is having the authority to make the decisions for Key Objectives and Metrics which impact the accomplishment of the mission of the company or firm.

Line Accountability is normally the function of the line departments and line managers who are directly accountable for accomplishing the Key Objectives of the company or firm. (See Accountability, Staff)

Accountability, Requirements for

There are three absolute requirements that define Accountability: 1) it is the offering of the <u>responsibilities</u> or fixed duties of work, 2) along with the <u>authority</u> given by a higher level to complete the work, and 3) accepted or agreed-to by the individual who is offered the work and authority.

In a management process, there must be all three requirements fulfilled in order to have true accountability, and accountability is the basis for any management process within a firm or company.

Accountability, Staff

Is having the authority for fully supporting the line departments and managers in accomplishing the mission of the company or firm.

The most successful companies and firms are those that have the best staff managers or partners who implement staff accountability to the Nth degree, not the best Line managers or partners. (See Manager, Line; Manager, Staff)

Accrued Authority

To increase or accumulate authority over some area of an organization by natural growth, such that the level of accountability is disjointed within a normal organization structure.

In management, accrued authority usually occurs when a manager or partner receives authority for one fixed duty or work, and maintains that authority over that work when the manager or partner is promoted to another position or level in the organization. It is a violation of the rules of organizing but occurs often in companies.

Acculturation of Management

The modification of the management culture of an organization or group of managers as a result of bringing accountability into the process of management.

The process of acculturation occurs in a company or firm when a CEO or Managing Partner recognizes that certain managers or partners are not achieving objectives according to agreed-upon metrics. The CEO or Managing Partner then implements the requirements of accountability in their management process, which heretofore had not been utilized. Acculturation of Management can also occur when the mission of the company is not being achieved by the CEO or Managing Partner, and the Board of Directors or Executive Committee directs the requirements of accountability to be implemented. (See Accountability, Requirements for)

Activities of Management (See, Segments of Management)

Administer Responsibilities

To manage the fixed duties of work and be responsible for managing that work.

In a management process to administer the work implies that the individual has the responsibility to manage the work but does not have the authority from a higher level to be accountable for any objectives, metrics, or decisions on that work. (See Responsibility)

Advise

To provide counsel or understanding of a problem or issue within an organization or team so that the real problem may be identified in logical decision making.

Advising is a normal activity of staff departments and staff individuals to the line departments and line individuals, but the concept of advising also relates to employees of a department advising the manager of that department. Advise does not require any level of authority to provide to managers at any level.

Advisory Board

Is a body of appointed members from outside the confines of the company or firm whose experience, expertise and sageness provide advice and service to the CEO or Managing Partner of the company or firm on an ongoing basis.

An Advisory Board is not an official unit of the company or firm, but is an external body that is normally formed when a company or firm has a passive board of directors or executive committee. We see these Advisory Boards normally in family owned businesses or smaller partnerships, where the board of directors is normally family members who do not provide the CEO with active participation. An Advisory Board is normally made up of confidants of the CEO or Managing Partner whose experience in management work trumps the experience in specialist work.

Agreement in Accountability

The act of accepting the work and responsibilities from a higher level of authority, along with the authority to complete the work and responsibilities, forming a new level of accountability within the organization.

Agreement is the third requirement for having real accountability within a department or organization, and without any agreement by the individual offered the work and responsibility there can be no accountability by that individual for that work, and the accountability remains at the higher level of authority. (See Accountability, Requirements for)

Analogous Practicality

Understanding the functions of management through practice or action, rather than theory, with results evolving from practice on the job in real time.

In a management process, analogous practicality occurs when a manager or partner develops a process of utilizing the activities of management within the organization and implements these as best practices for the organization. By doing so, it shows how to achieve objectives and metrics of the manager or partner's department or organization by working as an analogous team.

Analyze

To examine a problem or issue methodically and rationally by separating the problem or issue into parts or basic principles so as to determine the real problem to resolve.

In logical decision making, a manager or partner analyzes the apparent problem by asking who, what, where, why, when, and how, which will normally lead to the separation of the apparent problem from the real problem, and a decision can be made to resolve the real problem not the symptom, which is the apparent problem.

Apparent Problem (See Problem, Apparent)

Appraisal

The subjective role of the manager or partner in determining how the work was performed, not whether the work was performed and accomplished.

Appraisal is one of the most misunderstood concepts in the activity of Evaluation & Appraisal. Appraisal is an activity of the control function of management that occurs on a subjective basis by the manager or partner. It is not the objective evaluation of whether the work was performed to prescribed metrics, but the subjective side of how the work was performed. In managing in the 21st Century, evaluation of the work is the accountability of the subordinate accountable for accomplishing the work to standard or metric, and the Appraisal is the accountability of the manager or partner. (See Evaluation, Self)

Approval

To officially consent or confirm a certain type of work with the metrics required to complete the work.

The process of management requires that a manager of higher authority approve the objectives and metrics of the lower level of management or employees, so that the objectives of higher levels of management cascade or drill down to lower levels. This process starts with the Mission Statement of the company or firm and is driven initially by the Board of Directors to the President (or Executive Committee to the Managing Partner), and down to managers and partners of other departments, and then to lower levels of the organization, insuring that the mission is homogenous to the organization. (See Cascading of Objectives)

Art of Management

The conscious utilization of a system of axioms and techniques employed in the performance of management tenets requiring the exercise of prescient faculties that can only be learned by study, practice, and experience.

Management work is the hardest of work, whereas specialist work is the easiest of work because that is where an employee first excels. The art of management dictates that if an individual desires to become a key executive of the firm or company, he or she must study and understand the functions of management and their activities first, and then utilize them arduously every day in managing others. This can best be accomplished when a partner or manager understands AXIOMs of management that relate to these functions. (See also, Science of Management; Axiom)

Aspect of the Problem

In decision making, the manner in which a problem that is impacting the accomplishment of objectives and metrics is viewed by the mind.

Aspects of the Problem usually reflect a "doer" type of manager or partner because it is the manager's mind and not the team or department's mind. However, it is a good example of why in determining the real problem from the apparent problem, that using the minds of the entire team make for better decision making. Decision Making is an activity of the Leading function of management. (See Technique of Sound Decision Making)

Assessment of Alternatives

In the process of decision making, an <u>assessment of the alternatives</u> identifies the various work and action that occurs prior to the logical decision being made by a manager or partner.

This assessment of alternatives allows the manager or partner to determine the work and tactics that will provide the highest degree of success for the decision. Decision Making is an activity of the Leading function of management.

Assignment

To select an individual for a particular responsibility or objective.

In a management process, assignment designates a particular work or responsibility for an individual that achieves a designed objective according to preset and agreed metrics.

Assistant Manager (Partner)

Any individual who provides support and service to the manager or partner of the organization or department.

An assistant is <u>always</u> considered to be a staff role, regardless if the unit of assistance is a line or staff unit. As such, an assistant is never <u>accountable</u> for the objectives of the unit, but is always accountable for fully supporting and servicing the manager or partner who is.

Associate Manager (Partner)

Any individual who has been assigned the responsibility and authority for the objectives of a higher manager or unit of organization, and has agreed to complete the responsibility according to predetermined metrics.

An associate is <u>always</u> considered to be a line role, regardless if the unit is a line or staff unit. As such, an associate is always <u>accountable</u> for the objectives which she has agreed to complete according to the metrics provided by the manager or partner. (See Manager, Line)

Assumed Authority

The supposition by a manager or partner that full authority from a higher level has been provided to complete a responsibility or task, when in fact no authority has actually been provided by a higher level.

Assumed Authority is not always a bad situation, and most often it occurs in a company or firm when a higher level manager or partner is indecisive and procrastinating in decision making such that dependent accountabilities of lower levels cannot move forward. When an individual is initially hired, Assumed Authority usually accompanies the responsibilities described in the job description for that position. (See Job Description)

Assumptions of Strategy

The strategic suppositions approved by a CEO or Managing Partner in a company or firm that are considered to be probable in future stages of operational success. In the first function of management, Strategy, assumptions are determined which impact the current and future driving force(s) of the organization or unit, and are particularly important in developing the long term strategic initiative of the organization or unit. Assumptions of Strategy occur in strategic management and are conceived in the present but designed for the future.

Audit, Financial

An examination of financial records and accounts to determine their accuracy.

Financial audits usually occur on an annual basis, and are normally the responsibility of a Certified Public Accountant who will verify the accuracy according to formal accounting standards.

Audit of Management Tenets

An examination of an organization's use of the six functions and segments of management through the annual use of a management survey which identifies the strengths and weaknesses of the management team within these six functions.

Successful firms and companies consistently audit their management teams on an annual basis. Epic Management Group provides an all-encompassing survey called the Management Health Check which is taken by all employees of the organization. The results of the survey are compared versus the average results of companies in a database as well as comparison of the company's results year-to-year. A survey of how the employees view overall management techniques goes far to help the manager or partner.

Authority

The official capacity of a manager or partner to exercise total control over the actions of individuals within the company or firm in any responsibility or work.

Authority and use of authority in a management process is how successful companies establish accountability at lower levels of the firm or company. By definition, accountability involves the three ingredients: the work, the authority, and the agreement of the individual. (See Accountability, Requirements for; see Management Authority)

Authority, Assumed (See Assumed Authority)

Authority, Line of (See Line of Authority)

Authority, Objective

Authority which is always determined in writing, and always shown in formal /written communications within the organization.

Objective authority is used by managers whenever there are formal plans of the organization where each individual who is accountable for a part of the formal plan has been officially denoted as having accepted accountability for that part of the formal plan, and it is denoted in writing who is accountable for its accomplishment. In particular, Objective Authority is utilized by CEOs and Managing Partners in determining those individuals accountable for achieving the Strategic Action Plans within a Strategic Plan, and not accountable at lower levels of the organization. (See Strategic Action Plans; and Strategic Plan)

Authority, Subjective

Authority which is more appropriate for use in the spoken language than in the written language. In business, subjective authority would occur in informal communications.

Subjective authority is used in managing operationally on a daily basis where the title and position of the manager or partner implies the authority to make all decisions for which the manager or partner is accountable.

Authorize

The act of a manager or partner giving permission or approval for lower levels of the organization to take action to accomplish an objective.

In a management process, based upon the objective, both Subjective Authority and Objective Authority are utilized by a manager or partner. (See Authority, Objective; Authority, Subjective)

Axiom

In a management process, an Axiom is a sound principle that has been proven by ongoing evidence in the marketplace over a period of time concerning a defined activity of management.

Axioms in business are self-evident principles that have been proven by actual managers and partners over a period of years, and not a part of unproven concepts of theory developed by academia. (See Management Tenet)

"The two most valuable Leadership Management Tenets that must be mastered by a CEO or Managing Partner are accountability and managing with metrics."

Greg Weismantel

Vocabulary & Axioms for Professional Managers and Partners
2nd Edition © Gregory N. Weismantel, 2014

B

Board of Directors

Is a body of elected or appointed members of a company or corporation who oversee the activities of the President/CEO and are fully accountable for the mission of the company. The Board of Directors is always considered a staff unit to support the President/CEO.

The Objective Authority of a board of directors comes from the shareholders who elect them by vote, or from officers of the organization who appoint them. (See Board of Directors, Delegation; Authority, Objective).

Board of Directors, Advisory (See Advisory Board)

Board of Directors, Accountabilities

When the shareholders provide the authority for the board to perform its responsibilities, and the board members agree to perform those duties, there is a formal board accountability that is established for the mission of the company.

The accountabilities of a board of directors are staff accountabilities to support the CEO of the company or firm.

Board of Directors, Delegation

The Board of Directors is authorized to act as representatives for the shareholders of the company, and as such is accountable to the shareholders for achieving the Mission of the company. The Board then delegates the responsibility for the Mission to the President/CEO, along with the Objective Authority to the President/CEO to accomplish the Mission.

In a management process of a company, firm, or corporation, the President/CEO or Managing Partner is accountable to a higher level for the mission of the company, firm, or corporation. This higher level is a Board of Directors of a corporation or an Executive Committee of Partners for Managing Partner of a firm, which delegates the authority for the CEO or Managing Partner to take action.

Board of Directors, Responsibilities

The responsibilities of the board are typically determined by the organization's bylaws but are always driven by the President/CEO of the company.

Boards of Directors are either active or passive in nature. An active board will have board members who provide ongoing support and service to the President/CEO on an ongoing basis without being asked; a passive board usually provides little support and service to the President/CEO. Normally family owned businesses have passive boards, while public companies have active boards. There is no logic for this anomaly. (See, Advisory Board)

Bonus, Employee

Usually applies to money in excess of what is normally received or strictly due as wages for work performed, given in consideration of superior achievement or as a share in profits.

Companies and firms utilize a bonus as a short term incentive for individuals to be motivated to achieve added objectives which benefit the company or firm on a short term basis (See Motivation, Bonus Use; Motivation, Money Use)

Bonus, Performance

Usually applies to money in excess of what is normally received or strictly due as wages for work performed, given in consideration for achieving a set level of quality work determined by pre-agreed metrics.

Performance bonuses are often used the wrong way, merely as a sum of money to motivate the employee similar to a simple employee bonus. Performance bonuses should always be agreed-to before the responsibility or work is identified, and include agreed upon metrics that both the manager or partner and the employee have determined quantitatively (i.e., 16 barrels in 32 hours). (See Metrics)

Brainstorm

The steps in the process of problem solving by a department or team, where shared problem solving techniques occur in which all members of the team spontaneously contribute ideas and alternatives within the process.

The Brainstorming activity has two objectives in the problem solving process: 1) to allow the members of the team or department to provide real alternatives to the problem; and, 2) to allow the manager to receive complete commitment from the department or team in resolving the problem. The second alternative is the more important to the manager or partner, as the problem solving becomes the team's work.

Break-Even Point

In a management process, it is a financial analysis involving revenue, volume, and fixed & variable costs that is utilized by a CEO or Managing Partner to determine the proper head count (fixed cost) to support the profit level of the firm or company.

The Break-Even Point is a tool which managers and partners utilize in restructuring their organization. (See Axiom of Restructuring Objectives)

Budget

A monetary scheme in a company or firm for allotting planned expenses for a given period of time.

In a company or firm's management process, the budgets for the organization or the departments provide areas of control where metrics should be utilized to determine performance criteria for evaluation and appraisal (activities of the Control function of management). Budgets are an activity of the Planning function.

Budgeting Scheme

To plan in advance the expenditures of money for resources for a given period of time by the managers or partners of the company or firm.

Budgeting is an activity of the Planning function of management, which combines with the Control function of management using metrics to determine the success or failure of managers and partners to maintain a profit based upon the expenses of the profit formula. (See Profit; Profit Formula; Profit Sharing)

Bureaucracy

An administrative process in a company or firm in which the need to follow complex or outdated procedures stymies effective action to achieve the mission.

Ongoing Committees are examples of bureaucracies within a firm or company, as they stymie decisiveness. (See Committee)

Bureaucrat

A manager or partner of a company or firm who insists on rigid adherence to rules, routines and metrics that stifle the creativity and innovativeness of the organization.

In a management process of a firm or company, the line managers of operations are normally the violators of rigid adherence to rules, formulas, routines and metrics because the bureaucracy restricts their ability to achieve their objectives (i.e., sales, income revenue, profits) while staff managers are normally the originators of rules, formulas, and routines. Companies with unions also have union stewards that often add additional rules, formulas, and routines that restrict the efficient operation of the company. Successful companies recognize the importance to eliminate the bureaucratic rules that restrict the line units from achieving their objectives, while maintaining productive rules, formulas, routines and metrics that provide unrestricting parameters.

Business Units

The arranging of specific products and services of a company or firm into formal entities which operate within the core processes of the parent company, while having specific profit and loss accountability within their own unit of business.

Organizing a company or firm into Business Units is an activity of the Organizing function of management, and is normally associated with a matrix style organizational structure. Such an organizational structure is ineffective without total use of metrics and accountability by its managers and partners. (See Matrix Organization)

"Whenever you hear the words, 'we have a communications problem around here,' throw up a flag. It normally means the manager or partner is not planning properly with the team."

Greg Weismantel

C

Cascading of Objectives

A succession or series of processes of setting objectives with metrics, the output of each of which serves as the input for the next level, and which the originating manager or partner setting objectives drills down the objectives from higher to lower units of the organization.

In a management process, cascading of objectives from higher units of accountability to lower units of accountability is critical to the success of the organization in achieving its mission, because the mission is the accountability of the CEO/President and Managing Partner. (Also see Drill Down of Objectives)

Coach

A person who provides private instructions on a specific type of specialist or management work within an organization.

Coaching was all the craze of the consultant field during the early 2000's, prior to the great recession in 2008, when players were decimated with pink slips and coaches also lost their positions. The major problem with coaching in any field, including management, is that the number of excellent coaches is minimal while the number of poor to inadequate coaches is many.

Collaboration of Duties

The process of two disparate departments or organizations of a company or firm with different missions and objectives working together as a team in a joint effort of accomplishing a common objective.

Collaboration is an activity of the Teamwork function of management. While collaboration would appear to be an easy process to implement within a company or firm, in fact it is the most difficult because of the amount of commonality required of two disparate units, and the increased amount of continual communication required for success.

Collaborative Failure

The capability of a partner or manager to provide collaborative strategy and plans based upon having failed at achieving an objective with metrics over a period of time.

The success of J.C. Penny is the epitome example of collaborative failure in that he was often reported as saying he and his team failed in seven businesses before becoming successful and with each failure he eliminated the tactics which were the cause of it.

Command Authority

A manager or partner having the authority to dictate the manner and process by which an organization or individuals of the organization achieve objectives.

While Command Authority implies that the manager or partner makes all the decisions in a centralized manner, the Professional Manager or Partner of the 21st Century delegates this authority for decision making down to lower levels utilizing metrics to control the manner in which lower level individuals make the decisions.

Commitment

In a management process, commitment is the act of managers and partners being bound to a particular course of action, with an acknowledgement that the course of action will be implemented.

In the Planning function of management, commitment to achieving the objectives of a manager or partner occurs when the manager or partner allows his direct reports to have a say in the actions that will be taken to achieve the objectives. In this instance, the objectives become the work of the committed direct reports.

Committee

A bureaucratic group of people who do not have the formal authority (and accountability) to make a decision, but have the responsibility (the work) to determine the alternatives available for the person who does have the authority and accountability to make the decision.

A committee always has a staff accountability of support and service because it does not have the authority to make a decision. The person with the authority to make a decision has the line accountability over the committee. Many committees believe they have the authority to make a decision and therefore whenever a higher level of authority does not make the decision based upon a committee's recommendation, individuals on the committee become less enthused and motivated to belong to other committees. They do not understand their staff accountable role. (See Accountability, Staff)

Communicating Efficiently

To express oneself in such a way that the originator of the message is readily and clearly understood by the receptor of the message so that a response is relevant to the originating message.

Communication is an activity of the <u>Leading</u> function of management, and the best line and staff managers and partners are also the best communicators of their objectives and metrics. This allows the subordinates to easily understand the objectives and metrics and eliminates the need for them to ask several times what the manager or partner communicating the objective or responsibility really wants to achieve.

Communication in Teamwork

The amount of communication that is required for a team to accomplish its objective.

When the responsibilities performed require high amounts of information flow between units, then a high degree of communication and teamwork must occur; when the team requires low or no amounts of information flow between units the work might be completed with a low degree of communication and teamwork.

Communication, One-Way

By definition of communication, one-way communication is not officially communication with a receptor, but is a one-way issuance of responsibilities by an originator to a receptor without receiving any input of reception.

One-Way Communication is common in new managers or supervisors, who achieve objectives based upon their own ability and expertise as opposed to those of others, and is a violation of AXIOM of Management of Achieving Objectives. Perhaps a better example of this is inside a family with teen-agers, where the father or mother is speaking to their son or daughter and there is little response in return.

Communication, Two-Way

The process of sending and receiving messages from an originator to a receptor utilizing any device that will accommodate written, verbal, or digital messages.

In managing an organization, it is important that the CEO or Managing Partner understands that communication does not occur unless there is some type of response or verification of the message being received by the receptor. Thus, it is critical in communicating the mission, objectives, and metrics during the cascading process, that the CEO or Managing Partner insists that formal acknowledgement of receipt has occurred by lower level managers and partners. Is an email considered one-way or two-way communications? Communication is an activity of the Leading function of management.

Company

A formal organization which has a mission which provides products and services to other organizations as well as to the consuming public.

There are several types of companies: single proprietary companies owned by an individual; limited liability companies which take the form of a corporation but have several individuals working together within the company; corporations, both Sub-Chapter S corporations which operate as a corporation with a board of directors and stockholders but the profits are taxed to the individual stockholders; a C corporation, which operates as a corporation with a board of directors and stockholders and the profits are taxed to the corporation; a firm or partnership, where the owners, normally partners, are usually a limited liability company.

Conclusion

In formal decision making, a conclusion is a judgment made after a discussion of all the alternatives related to resolving the real problem.

Conclusions occur prior to the final decision of what action to take to resolve the real problem. Conclusions are an activity of decision making, and precede all problem solving and action planning events because the conclusion process includes differentiating the apparent problem from the real problem in a formal decision making technique. (See Technique of Sound Decision Making)

Conduct, Management

The way a manager or partner acts or behaves in his managerial capacity.

There is an unwritten code of Management Conduct which insists that a manager or partner acts as the leader of the organization, not as a follower. This includes ethics, appearance, and other qualities that set the position of manager or partner above the common level of importance.

Consolidation, Organization

The merger of two or more organizations with different missions and objectives to form one organization with a unified mission and objectives.

Organization consolidation normally occurs when two companies or departments merge during a restructuring of the organization, or in a merger & acquisition procedure.

Consultant

A person who gives expert advice on a particular area of knowledge, based upon his experience and expertise within a broad general area of knowledge or a specific area of knowledge.

Consultants should all have credentials of having worked with a mentor consultant firm or individual consultant who has the area of expertise and knowledge in which he or she consults with clients. Without such mentoring, the expertise of the consultant is always in question.

Consultant, Management

A person who gives expert advice in the management area of knowledge as it relates to the functions of managing a company or firm.

A Management Consultant receives his knowledge of management through being a manager during his career, and not from academia where management theory is taught. Normally a Management Consultant has been an executive or CEO, or Managing Partner with one or several firms or companies that provide on the job experiences in management tenets.

Control

A Function of Management. It is a metric of comparison for measuring or verifying the results of an objective or unit of work.

A manager or partner utilizes the function of control so that there are guidelines or parameters that allow their subordinates to take action without having the manager or partner do so. (**See Function of Management, Control**)

Control by the 20/80 Rule (Exception)

The process of evaluating an individual's performance in achieving objectives by spot checking (inspecting) ongoing work results as opposed to inspecting each activity of the individual. Also called Control by Exception.

Utilizing the 20/80 rule, inspect the critical few factors and not the un-critical many. Professional managers and partners utilize control by the 20/80 rule and achieve many objectives through and with the team; first line supervisors and "doer" managers and partners inspect every single widget and achieve fewer ongoing objectives. (See, AXIOM of Management Accomplishment)

Control by the 80/20 Rule (Inspection)

The process of evaluating an individual's performance in achieving objectives by inspecting each activity of the individual's ongoing work results as opposed to spot-checking the critical few. Also called Control by Inspection.

The opposite of Control by the 20/80 Rule, and usually is found in the managerial traits of a "doer" manager or partner who achieves objectives through his own expertise and knowledge. Control by inspection is when each widget must be observed for quality by the manager or partner, often called micro-managing in management terms.

Coordination, External

The process of harmonious interaction formed by joining independent individuals and departments within an organization, and/or individuals and departments outside the organization, together in a team.

External Coordination is an activity of the Teamwork function of management, and usually occurs on large projects where an external 3rd Party company or firm is required to supplement an organization's knowledge skill sets. External coordination is the most difficult tactic to implement across company lines.

Coordination, Internal

The process of harmonious interaction formed by joining independent individuals and departments within an organization together into a team.

Internal Coordination occurs on smaller projects and more often than External Coordination, and is an activity of the Teamwork function of management. Internal coordination is the less difficult tactic to implement across company lines.

Core Process

Any process of the organization which is utilized to accomplish the Mission and Key Objectives of the company, firm, department, or individual.

Successful firms, companies, and departments all have formal graphs of their Core Processes with accountabilities available for all individuals to know and understand. Determining the Core Processes of a company or firm is normally the first order of business for a newly hired CEO or Managing Partner, because the Core Processes identify the accountabilities of departments along with the organizational structure of the individuals of the company or firm. It is not unusual for a newly appointed or hired CEO or Managing Partner to analyze the operational Core Processes within the first month of tenure.

Critical Factors

In planning, the Critical Factors are essential to the accomplishment of an objective; they are key conditions of the essence to an objective.

The "critical factors" as opposed to the "uncritical factors" are the adages for managers and partners in the 21st century, when resources are at a minimum.

Critical Few Factors

The 1-3 factors which are the most important ingredients to accomplishing the objective, and can be in the conditions of the objective or metrics of an objective.

The "critical few factors" as opposed to the "uncritical many factors" are the adages for managers and partners in the 21st century, when resources are at a minimum. This is sometimes referred to as the critical few factors versus the uncritical many factors and they utilize AXIOMs of Pareto's Constant (20/80 Rule). (See Uncritical Many Factors)

Culture of the Company or Firm

The totality of a firm or company's beliefs and traditions and any other characteristic of a company or firm's business environment.

Every company or firm has its own culture usually based upon the founder of the business, and what behavior patterns emanated during the company or firm's formative years. The culture of the company is one of the most important factors involved in the Organizing function of management, particularly in the activity and process of hiring an individual. (Also see, Acculturation of Management)

"A Board of Director's performance is only as good as the performance of its CEO, because a Board of Directors is a staff unit, which must support and serve the CEO in accomplishing the mission. The same can be said of the Executive Committee of a Partnership and the Managing Partner. And if they are not supporting the CEO or Managing Partner.......FIRE YOUR BOARD!"

Greg Weismantel

D

Decide

The act by which a manager or partner determines the conclusion in a definite manner, without a doubt.

Managers and partners have the ultimate accountability to decide in a resolute manner, free from hesitation or vacillation. Not doing so causes hesitation in taking action for achieving objectives on the part of the subordinates.

Decision

The act of reaching a conclusion on the alternatives available for a manager to take action.

In professional management for the 21st Century, managers and partners must achieve more objectives with fewer subordinates, and making a decision by the team requires complete accountability for the most productive teams and organizations.

Decision Making, Centralized

The assignment of power and authority to bring all decisions under a centralized leadership in an organization so that decisions are made by a single, central authority.

Centralized decision making normally occurs at two levels of an organization: 1) with managers and partners who are doers and want to hold onto all authority to make every decision; and 2) older managers and partners who always demonstrate resistance to change. Management in the 21st century requires all managers and partners to drive decision making down to lower levels of the organization, but this requires also driving down the authority to lower levels. That is usually the sticking point with some managers and partners.

Decision Making, Decentralized

To delegate the decision making functions and authority for achieving objectives from a central authority to lower level employees of the organization.

Decentralized decision making is the key process of managing for the 21st century, where organizations are flat and employees wear many hats. The critical function of management to accomplish this is Control, and the use of agreed-to metrics for taking action. When a manager or partner does not utilize metrics to delegate objectives or work, it opens his position up to unexpected consequences, which are seldom good for the manager or partner.

Decision Making, Logical

Logical Decision Making is using logic and reasoning in a systematic fashion to come to a decision with a team.

Logical Decision Making includes gathering the facts from the team members themselves and making a logical decision based upon the member's input, which is the best trait of a professional partner or manager. Logical Decision Making is always the best method when a team or group of managers or partners is working together to solve a problem or issue. The reason is because it allows the Managing Partner or CEO to facilitate the process while the participants make a commitment to achieving what is decided.

Decision Making, Natural

Natural Decision Making is that decision which usually stems from a manager or partner having a special proficiency being able to make an immediate decision, based upon innate ability and knowledge of the job.

Natural Decision Making is seen more often in the entrepreneurial environment as well as in first line management positions, and less frequently in upper management decision making. "Gut Feeling" is a term often used for natural decisions. There are times when Natural Decision Making is a good process, but not when a team or group of diverse people or departments is involved in the decision making process.

Decisive

When a manager or partner has the authority to make a decision, and is observed as being firm and resolute in using that authority for reaching a conclusion.

Decision making is an activity of the Leadership function of management, and being decisive in decision making is a strong leadership trait to direct reports, who are most observant about the characteristics of the partner or manager to whom they report.

Definition

The act of stating a precise meaning or significance of a word, phrase or term as used by managers and partners in setting objectives and metrics.

The Strategy, Planning, and Control functions of management all require complete definition of objectives and metrics related to Strategic and Operational Management.

Delegate

To authorize an individual within an organization to accomplish a fixed body of work or responsibility, properly given with metrics.

The individual does not have to be a member of the same organization or at the same managerial level to have work delegated with authority. In fact, this process can be utilized to delegate up the organization to higher levels as well as lower levels, but with great sensitivity. Delegation and accountability are related in that they both have the work, authority, and agreement but delegation also has metrics, which allows the measurement of the accomplishment.

Delegation

The act of authorizing a person to accomplish a particular work or responsibility along with metrics required to measure accomplishment of the work, and with full agreement by the individual receiving the work, metrics, and authority to complete that work.

Delegation is exactly like accountability in regards to establishing another level of accountability. Even though the work has been delegated down to a lower level of individual in the organization, the manager or partner who delegates the work remains accountable to a higher level for its accomplishment according to metrics. (See Accountability, Definition of)

Delegator Manager (See Manager, Delegator)

Delineation of Management Levels

To develop the distinction between the four levels of management (first line, middle, executive, and general) as it relates to specific accountabilities for objectives and metrics of the organization.

Delineation of Management Levels is important in the cascading or drill-down process of bringing objectives and metrics from higher to lower levels in the organization, from General Managers to Executive Managers to Middle Managers and to First Line Managers. (See Cascading of Objectives; Drill Down of Objectives)

Developing Direct Reports

An ongoing accountability of each partner or manager who has individuals reporting to them, and whose authority is often usurped by training activities of staff departments.

Developing Direct Reports is a line management accountability, not a staff management accountability. It is not the same as training direct reports. Training is 90% driven by the company or firm, where staff departments are accountable for the training programs of employees, and 10% driven by the individual; development is 10% driven by the company or firm and 90% driven by the individual.

Development, Manager

In management, to progress from simpler to more complex stages of managing a firm, business, department, or team.

The four stages of Manager Development are as follows: first line supervisor, to middle manager, to executive manager, to general manager. There is very little training involved in Manager Development, as 90% of the development falls on the desire and drive of the individual to achieve each complex stage, not the company. (See Training)

Direct Reports

Those individuals who report directly to a higher level of management of the organization and who are accountable for the work and responsibility of that higher level.

The Direct Reports of a successful manager or partner in the 21st Century must recognize that accountability is different than responsibility, and that delegating the responsibility of a manager or partner demands the utilization of accountability with metrics. Accountability is an activity of the Leading function of management; a Metric is an activity of the Control function of management. (See Function of Management, Leadership; Function of Management, Control; Management Process)

Directive Statement

An order or instruction issued by a manager or partner for an individual, department, or team to take action on a particular work or responsibility.

A Directive Statement is only one part of the process of defining the accountability that must occur to accomplish an objective. A Directive Statement does not include the process of planning nor the inclusion of relevant metrics which are essential in solving the real problem and not the apparent problem.

Divisions, Corporate

The arranging of specific products and services of a company or firm into formal entities which operate within their own core processes of management.

Normally only large companies and firms break down their products and services into Divisions. Smaller companies break down their products and services into Business Units. (See Business Units)

Drill Down of Objectives

The process by which a manager or partner of an organization determines the critical objectives of achievement required to achieve the mission of the company or firm, and forces these objectives unequivocally to lower units through the process of cascading objectives to lower levels of the organization.

Drill down of objectives is not a negative connotation of empowerment whatsoever. Quite often within an organization a particular manager or partner is like a rock in inhibiting the process of cascading the proper objectives down to lower levels, and it often is necessary for a CEO or Managing Partner of a higher level to force these objectives down through the rock-like level of manager by drilling them down. (Also see, Cascading Objectives)

Driving Force(s)

Is the specialist areas of the company or firm which dictate its reason for being, and is the primary determinant of the scope of your products, services, and markets. They are the factors which drive the business to be what it is and they are the determining factors for the scope of future products, services and markets.

Driving forces emanate from strategic areas of the company, are usually determined by Vision, Competition, Customer Persona, Products and Markets, Internal Resources & skill sets, and the External Environment.

Driving Force, Current

The primary determinant of the current scope of your products, services, or markets, and which drives the commitments of the mission of the company.

The following strategic areas usually "drive" a company or firm: Products/Services you sell; Market needs; Technology or Systems; Sales Processes; Marketing; Distribution; Resources available; Growth; Profit/ROI; and Production. Each of the above dictate a different method of operation to achieve the strategy of the company.

Driving Force, Future

The primary determinant of the future scope of your products, services, or markets.

When the final decision about any future product or service, or entering any future market is made, the Driving Force is dictated by one of these strategic areas shown in the Current Driving Force definition.

"…If you don't know where you're going, then any road will take you there."

Alice in Wonderland
Lewis Carroll

E

Elementary Tenets

In management, Elementary Tenets pertain to the fundamental or essential characteristics of management tenets as found in principles and axioms.

Axioms in Management Tenets are elementary to the process of managing. Understanding and utilizing AXIOMs allow the manager and partner to develop through the four stages of management development. (See Development, Management)

Empowerment

Empowerment is the process by which managers and partners enable their direct reports to <u>have the full authority to take action</u> when engaging with other people or departments <u>where no formal accountability has been established</u>.

The concept of "empowerment" became fashionable during the recession of the late 1900's, when companies had reduced head count and utilized teams in a matrix type of organization to achieve objectives. Often this situation is called empowerment because heretofore an employee or a department did not have this authority to take action. Empowerment without utilizing metrics places the manager or partner in an area of great risk. (See Accountability, Definition of)

Enterprise, Business

An organization of business which has some scope within an industry, with complications and risk associated with that business, and which overcomes those complications and risk by developing a management process which includes a formal mission that is accomplished by a CEO or Managing Partner through the utilization of objectives and metrics.

A management process requires the same objectives and metrics which accomplish the mission of the enterprise to be drilled-down or cascade to lower levels of the organization so that the team and organization are addressing a related objective.

Enterprising

That trait of a CEO or Managing Partner that shows imagination, creativity, and innovation to undertake a business venture that is acknowledged having complications and risk.

The most successful enterprising companies and firms, small and large, have formal (written) plans and measurements of those plans that are communicated down throughout the organization, reducing the amount of complication and risk involved to the CEO or Managing Partner.

Environment, Business External

The combination of external physical conditions that affect the creative growth and development of products and services of a company or firm, and which is an important step in developing strategy.

Some factors in the Business External Environment are: the economy, market, technology, political, legal, and competition that influences the manner in which the customers, suppliers, vendors and competitors impact the driving force of the company or firm. (See Driving Forces)

Environment, Business Internal

The combination of internal physical conditions that affect and influence the capability for growth within an organization.

This is an activity of the Strategy function of management which requires thorough analysis by the CEO and Managing Partner in developing a strategic plan. Key areas of the Business Internal Environment include: Organization and Management; Services, Products, Facilities; Information Technology; Finance; Marketing and Sales.

Evaluation

In a management process, whenever a manager or partner ascertains the accomplishment of a certain responsibility of work to determine an individual's level of performance in accomplishing that work.

Inherent in this definition is the assumption that there is a measurement, a metric, in which the individual has preset the accepted level of performance. Both metrics and evaluation are activities and segments of the Control function of management.

Evaluation, Manager (Partner)

The process by which a manager or partner determines a subordinate's level of performance in achieving his objective(s) according to a measurement (metric).

Manager (or Partner) Evaluation is a segment or activity of the Control function of management. Prior to 2008 and the great recession, Manager or Partner Evaluation was an activity of the management process of a company or firm. However with the coming of the great recession, companies and firms no longer had an abundance of doer managers so that self-evaluation is now the process commonly utilized by companies and firms for the 21st

Century. However this requires that a manager or partner become adept in managing with metrics that are understood by the subordinate as well as the manager or partner. (See Evaluation, Self; Manager Doer; and Manager, Professional)

Evaluation, Self-

The process by which a partner or manager's subordinate determines his own level of performance in achieving his objective(s) according to a metric measurement agreed-to between the partner or manager and the subordinate prior to taking action on the objective(s).

Self-Evaluation is an activity of the Control function of management. Self-Evaluation by an individual of his own objectives allows the partner or manager to achieve more objectives through and with others, and is the basis for progressing to a Professional Manager from a Doer Manager in the 21st Century. (See Manager, Doer; and Manager, Professional)

Exception, Control by

(See Control by Exception; Control by the 20/80 Rule)

Exception, Metric

A measurement that does not conform to the normal rules of a manager's objectives. This occurs when conditions outside the manager's control dictate a different measurement than what would be considered the norm.

A Metric Exception occurs during self-evaluation, which is an activity of the Control function of management, when some unique happenstance has made the current metric that measures the performance of the manager or partner impossible to achieve. An example of this is when a product manager has a metric of purchasing a raw material at a certain measureable price, but then a drought occurs which prohibits any possible purchase at the measurable price.

Execution

In business, to perform or carry out what is required in a plan according to agreed-to metrics between a person of higher authority and a person of lower authority.

Execution occurs most often in the Planning function of management, where steps of a plan have an accountability associated with the authority given from a higher level to a lower level. Accountability for the completion of the entire plan, according to metrics, is the accountability of the team leader or department manager; but the completion of steps of the plan are delegated to other members of the team or department, creating a new level of accountability for those steps.

Executive Agreement

An agreement made between two executives of the same company or firm, who have managerial authority over two different segments of the business.

Executive Agreement occurs when two different executives or partners who are accountable for two different segments of business agree on an issue that impacts both segments. This infers that the agreement can only be related to what both executives are accountable, and nothing which falls outside of either executive's authority.

Executive Council

A team of executives of the same company or firm who advise or assist the CEO/President or Managing Partner on important and critical issues affecting the mission of the company or firm.

An Executive Council is a staff unit of the organization, which means that it does not have the authority (and accountability) to make a decision, but it has the full accountability to provide complete support and service to the CEO/President or Managing Partner who does have the authority to make the decision on the issue at hand.

Executive Decree

An authoritative order issued by an executive manager or partner usually enacted by a company, firm or department of whom the manager or partner is accountable; usually issued on the sole authority of an accountable manager or partner.

An Executive Decree cannot be issued by a committee or council (staff units) because of the lack of authority which those entities have within a company or firm. It also cannot be issued by any line unit manager or partner that is not authorized to do so by an executive with the authority of a higher level.

Executive Manager (Partner)

An individual in a company or firm who has managerial authority over a certain segment of the business.

Executive Managers are normally considered direct reports of the CEO of the company, or direct reports of the Managing Partner of a firm. (See Delineation of Management Levels)

Executive Primer Program

A development program for managers or partners that covers the basic elements of management work for which an executive is accountable.

An Executive Primer program is utilized as a base development program for middle managers in their quest to become executive managers.

Expectation

Refers to the probable occurrence of a certain level of performance by the individuals accountable for achieving the mission and key objectives of the company or firm: the Managing Partner or the CEO.

If expectations are not formalized with measurements (metrics) then the same problem of Management By Objective (MBO) occurs within the company or firm, and that proliferates conflict between levels of management and the employee's themselves.(See Proliferation, Negative; Proliferation, Positive; Management By Objectives)

Vocabulary & Axioms for Professional Managers and Partners
2nd Edition © Gregory N. Weismantel, 2014

"Most academia believe that 'leadership' is the most important function of the CEO or Managing Partner, but leadership is only effective when combined with strategy, planning, organizing, teamwork, and control, which is the difference between a CEO or Managing Partner and a leader."

Greg Weismantel

Feedback, Brainstorm

In the decision making & problem solving processes, Brainstorm Feedback is the spontaneous contribution of individuals addressing the real problem versus the apparent problem, along with determining the optimal course of action to resolving the real problem.

Brainstorm Feedback occurs as an activity of decision making and problem solving, which are activities of the Leading function of management. (See Brainstorm)

Follow Through

The act or process of increasing effectiveness of the results of a plan that has been conceived, formalized, and implemented by a department or team within the company or firm.

Whenever a formal, written project plan or action plan is developed by a team, the most critical responsibility is in making certain that the plan is completed according to the metrics of the plan. A critical role of a manager or partner is to follow through with the implementation of the steps of the plan according to agreed-to metrics (See Axiom of Adequate Follow-Through)

Forecasting

To estimate or calculate income and expenses before the event, as an advance indication of coming events or conditions within the company or firm.

Forecasting is an activity of the Planning function of management. While forecasting is prevalent in the financial area of a company or firm, it is also utilized as a prediction of metrics for objectives which are non-financial in nature.

Function of Management, Control

In a management process, Control is the act of assuring that performance will occur in the manner and with the results intended.

Control allows a manager or partner to measure the progress toward achievement of planned objectives and take corrective action where deviations from expected results occur.

Function of Management, Control Segments of Activities

All segments of activities associated with the Control Function of Management including the following: Axioms of Management; Metrics; Goal Setting; Key Performance Indicators (KPI); Objective Evaluation and Subjective Appraisal; Improving Work Performance and Results Achieved.

The function of Control is normally utilized with every other function of management and their segments of activities. The Control function of management is the most difficult for a partner or manager to master, but those who do normally become the Presidents, CEOs and Managing Partners of companies and firms.

Function of Management, Leading

The utilization of motivational and logical activities to enlist the aid and support of others in accomplishing an objective.

A leader is one who leads or guides others in accomplishing the mission, and a leader is not necessarily a manager or partner, nor has to be one to be a good leader. Whereas a manager or partner must be a leader, and by definition a manager must master the six (6) functions of management – of which Leading is a critical function. There is no evidence that training in leadership tenets creates a leader, but merely allows an individual to understand the traits of being a leader.

Function of Management, Leading Segments of Activities

All segments of activities associated with the Leading function of management. These include the following: Decision Making; Problem Solving; Communicating; Innovation; Motivation; Negotiation; Training & Development.

The Leading function of management normally operates in conjunction with activities of the Control function of management.

Function of Management, Organizing

To arrange the work of an organization in a coherent, orderly, and structured pattern, so that it can be accomplished in the most productive manner in achieving the objective or the mission of the company or firm.

Partners and managers in the 21st Century should always organize around the work, not around the people of the organization. Organizing around the people dictates that more assistants with the proper skill sets must be hired to support that partner or manager who does not have the skill set required to achieve a position's objectives. The Organizing function of management normally operates in conjunction with activities of the Teamwork function of management. For example, whenever a manager restructures a department utilizing accountability, he or she always identifies the line and staff functionality involved.

Function of Management, Organizing Segments of Activities

All segments of activities associated with the Organizing function of management. These include the following: Accountability; Responsibility; Delegation; Restructuring; Functional Grouping; Span of Control; Interviewing, People Selection, Hiring, Firing.

The functions of Teamwork (conflict resolution) and Leadership (training and development) are normally utilized in conjunction with Organizing Activities.

Function of Management, Planning

To formulate a scheme or program for the accomplishment or attainment of a manager or partner's objectives, or the mission of the organization.

The Planning function of management normally operates in conjunction with activities of the Control function of management. Whenever a manager or partner sets his or her objectives (Planning) a metric (Control) is always utilized.

Function of Management, Planning Segments of Activities

All segments of activities associated with the Planning function of management. These include the following: Strategic Planning; Operations Planning; Project Management Planning; Objective Setting; Scheduling; Budgeting; Forecasting; Creating Policies and Procedures; and preparing the Mission Statement.

The functions of Control (metrics) and Leadership (communication) are normally utilized in conjunction with planning activities.

Function of Management, Strategy

The science or art of management as applied to the overall planning and conduct of stratagem within ongoing business operations. The effective partner or manager must be a visionary in determining what series of stratagem and tactics will be utilized to beat the competition in the long term, not just annually.

The effectiveness of the Managing Partner or CEO in charge of implementing a formal strategy will dictate the success or failure of the business in the long term. (See Stratagem; Strategic Plan; Strategic Management)

Function of Management, Strategy Segments of Activities

All segments of activities associated with the Strategy function of management. These include the following: Vision; Driving Forces; Mission; Product/Service-Market Analysis; and Competitive Analysis

The functions of Control (Key Performance Indicators KPI) and Leadership (motivation and communication) are normally utilized in conjunction with Strategy Activities.

Function of Management, Teamwork

To take harmonious action in a unified or "team" effort for obtaining active help, cooperation, understanding, and agreement from another person, department or segment of the business, <u>over which there is no authority.</u>

Teamwork is important because rarely can a partner, manager, department or organization achieve its mission by itself. It requires the harmonious help and coordination of other people in other teams. However, even perfect teamwork and coordination will not guarantee success. Teamwork never works without the help of activities of other functions of management. In particular, activities in the functions of Organizing and Leading normally accompany Teamwork.

Function of Management, Teamwork Segments of Activities

All segments of activities associated with the Teamwork function of management. These include the following: Line & Staff Functional Relationships; Collaboration; Empowerment; Team Building; Internal & External Coordination; Conflict Resolution.

The functions of Control (metrics) and Organizing (accountability) are normally utilized in conjunction with Teamwork Activities.

Function, Work

The work or responsibility for which a person or thing is particularly fitted or employed to accomplish. It is a function of the specialist work that an individual learns in a particular skill set.

A Work Function is normally that skill that an individual brings to the job on the first day, and is a critical part of the selection process of the Organizing function of management. (See Cross Functional Training)

Functions of Leadership Management

The six most essential activities or functions of a leadership manager or partner, where one function is so related to another that for each segment of activity assumed by one function there is a related segment of activity determined by the other. Thus, one function of management never operates by itself.

The six most critical functions of a manager or partner are Strategy, Planning, Organizing, Leading, Teamwork, and Control, with each function having selected segments of activities associated with it.

"Lack of a plan or a bad plan are both signs of managerial incompetence."

Henri Fayol (1841-1925)

Game Changer Events

In strategy and strategic planning, Game Changer Events are significant undertakings by a company that impact its future products and services through a change in the company's driving force.

Whenever a company has a significant game changer event, it is one that impacts the forward direction of its products and services, and most often designates a review of the company's current and future driving force. "Game changers" are often utilized to move a company or firm from one market to multiple markets, or move products and services from one market to another.

Goal

In a management process, a Goal is the qualitative *description of the measurement that needs to be equalized or* *exceeded so that the metric of the objective is proven without* *a doubt.*

A Goal is not an objective, but is the qualitative description of what has to be exceeded in order for the metric and Key Performance Indicator (KPI) to prove that the objective is achieved. For example in football, the objective is to win the game; but moving down the field 100 yards and crossing the line is the qualitative goal. The quantitative description of the measurement is the six (6) points earned when crossing the goal line. Setting an objective is an activity of the Planning function of management;

while setting a Goal of the metric is an activity of the Control function of management.

Group

In a company or firm, a Group is a number of individuals, products/services, or things considered together because of similarity of attributes. A group of individuals does not have any authority to accomplish a common mission with objectives and metrics, similar to a committee.

There is no such thing as "group accountability" since by definition the authority which is given from a higher level of authority goes in a series of dots through one individual at a time to show who is accountable. A Group is not a team. (See Team)

Guide, Management

Any counseling or mentoring that helps a partner or manager to control and lead a segment of the operations of a company or firm through use of objectives with metrics.

A Management Guide could also come from books on the use of management techniques but is always influenced by the tenets of management from the six functions of management: Strategy, Planning, Organizing, Leading, Teamwork, and Control.

Habilitation, Management

In a management process, to disclose an ability or capacity to qualify for a managerial or partner position to a higher source of authority.

Management Habilitation is important in the amount of time that it takes to become or enter the next level of management. In the progression of a manager or partner through the four levels within a company or firm, the manager or partner must be proficient in achieving objectives with metrics, but at the same time must make his intentions of becoming a higher level manager or partner known to his superior so that a minimum amount of time occurs to reach those levels. (See Management Development; Management Training)

Habitual Techniques

Behaving or performing management work in a certain manner by habit, such that management tenets are a natural part of a partner or manager's modus operandi and successful techniques.

Habitual performance of management work includes the segments of activities of the six functions of management: Strategy, Planning, Organizing, Leading, Teamwork, and Control.

Habituated Management Tenets

To become accustomed to the blocking and tackling tenets of management by frequent use and repetition or prolonged exposure to the solid Tenets of Management utilized by successful companies and firms.

Successful managers and partners in the 21st Century are those who Habituate the Management Tenets of successful companies and firms, from utilizing objectives with metrics to tracing the line of authority to determining who is accountable for the responsibilities of the company or firm.

Half-Cocked Manager (or Partner)

A manager or partner who is inadequately prepared to manage an organization or team properly.

A Half-Cocked Manager or Partner does not feel that management work is important versus specialist work, and "handles" the business as opposed to "managing" it.

Hardball Manager (or Partner)

A manager or partner who uses any means, however ruthless, to attain an objective.

Hardball Managers and Partners have a difficult time working through and with direct reports, and are more apt to be Doer Managers such as occurs in the role of first line manager. (See Leadership Style; Manager, Doer)

Havoc, Organizational

Any organization whether a company, firm or department of such, which does not have a formal process of management where widespread management disorder occurs on an ongoing basis.

Regardless of the size of the company or firm, Organizational Havoc always occurs in a widespread manner when there is no formal management process that is formally implemented by the

CEO/President or Managing Partner, from his level all the way down to the lowest employee level of the organization. When Organizational Havoc occurs, each direct report of the CEO or Managing Partner has his own individual mission, which is not the same mission as the CEO or Managing Partner. (See Organization, Matrix)

Hierarchy, Business Organization

A level within a business organization that is organized or classified according to rank or authority for a set group of responsibilities to achieve the mission of the company or firm.

A traditional hierarchy of a company is in the tree formation, where functional groupings of work and skill sets occur at specific levels based upon the specialist work required to achieve the CEO's or Managing Partner's key objectives. A traditional hierarchy of a firm or partnership is in a matrix formation, which is the most difficult organizational structure to implement due to the fact that one individual of the firm has multiple bosses to whom he or she is accountable for specific work. A matrix organization can be the most productive type when a company or firm does not have significant manpower in particular skill sets to accomplish the objectives of a department, and must use the skill sets of other departments to do so.

"Whenever a manager or partner hears the cliché *'we have to be flexible around here,'* it is a direct reflection on management ineptness and indecisiveness, and should be considered by a manager or partner as a warning sign."

Greg Weismantel

Identifying Vital Signs

In the process of developing metrics, Identifying Vital Signs of the objective leads to the area where measurements are the most meaningful for self-evaluation and appraisal.

The vital signs of the human body are temperature, blood pressure, heartbeat, etc. and the metric for the vital signs are quantitative, such as 98.6 degrees Fahrenheit for temperature. Identifying the vital signs of an objective leads to the best metric that measures its accomplishment.

Input for Planning

In any planning process, input into the plan by the team or department is critical for the total implementation of the plan and achievement of the objective.

Who best to describe what actions are best to take than the workers who are most familiar with the process in the department. Secondly, when a manager or partner allows full input by her direct reports into the plan, there is a commitment to the plan by the team or department, and ownership of the objective swings from fully being the manager or partner's to also being the direct reports.

Interpretation, Work

A manager or partner's representation of the meaning of an objective or metric to a direct report so that the proper tactics will be utilized to achieve the objective.

In communicating the objective and the metric required for achieving the objective, clarity of message must occur with the workers who will perform the work. Work Interpretation occurs when the manager or partner becomes more specific about the tasks at hand and the metric of measurement expected.

Issue or Problem

In decision making, a point or matter of discussion leading to the final result or conclusion as a solution to the issue or problem.

This is an aspect of problem solving which leads to a formal Action Plan by the team or department accountable for resolving the issue or problem.

Issue or Problem, Apparent

The symptom to the issue or problem that a manager or partner first recognizes as the real problem prior to questioning and utilizing a formal decision making technique.

Whenever a manager or partner begins to resolve the Apparent Issue or Problem and does not pursue the Real Issue or Problem, wasted effort and wasted work occurs by the team in trying to resolve the symptom and not the Real Issue or Problem. Decision Making is an activity of the Leading function of management.

Issue or Problem, Real

The ultimate problem that a manager or partner resolves following a complete analysis of the apparent issues and problems along with a technique for rational team decision making.

When resolving the Real Problem, the manager or partner maintains his integrity for being a good decision maker with his or her direct reports because whenever you attempt to resolve the Apparent Problem or symptom, wasted effort occurs by the direct reports of a manager. If during this process of decision making the Apparent Problem is being worked on by the team, wasted effort occurs because the team is expending energy on resolving the symptom. It is during this time period that the words are often heard from the team, "we have to be flexible around here." These words have nothing to do with flexibility, but the ineptness of the manager or partner.

"...The bull loses to the matador, because it identifies the cape as *the Real Problem*, instead of the matador!"

Anonymous

Job Description

Is an overall listing of all the responsibilities which a position of employment requires an individual to perform in their ongoing daily tasks.

Note that because Job Descriptions do not include the amount of authority that the individual will receive when he accepts this job, there is by definition no accountability. However, presumed authority often accommodates the Job Description.

Job Enhancement

The process by which a manager or partner makes a job description more full and meaningful, and more rewarding so that the direct report remains motivated to achieve all objectives according to the proper metric.

Job Enhancement is a short term phenomenon which stimulates and motivates individual employees. A manager requires Manager Development to maintain his or her motivation to strive to become promoted to one of the four levels of manager. (See Delineation of Management Levels)

Job Knowledge

The state of knowing a job's specialist work requirements through familiarity, awareness, or understanding gained through experience or study, or training on the essential facets of the specialist work of the job description.

Job Knowledge reflects the level of skills which an individual has over time in performing the same job and is considered the basis for specialist work. (See Work, Specialist)

Job or Task

A specified work or responsibility that a partner or manager provides to their direct reports for accomplishing their portion of the cascaded or drilled-down objectives and metrics, from a higher level to their level.

Whenever an individual is delegated a specific job or work, inherent in that delegation should be the authority to do that work, and if not, the individual is responsible for doing the work but not accountable for the decisions to be made about that work. Accountability remains with a higher level.

K

Key Decision Point

Is the determining factor as to which course of action will be chosen from the list of alternatives developed in the Logical Decision Making process.

The Key Decision Point sorts through what should be done with what can be done.

Key Objectives and Metrics

Those ongoing objectives of a unit or individual that are the basis and reason for being a part of the organization. Key Objectives with metrics are the basis for evaluation and appraisal of an individual's performance.

In a management process, the key objectives and metrics of the CEO or Managing Partner reflect the accomplishment of the mission of the firm or company, and as such, the CEO or Managing Partner is accountable for achieving the mission, and he is accountable to the Board of Directors of the company or the Executive Partner Committee of the firm. (See Cascading of Objectives; Drill-Down of Objectives; Board of Directors; Board of Directors, Accountabilities)

Key Performance Indicators - KPI

A Metric with quantifiable attributes which represent an unmistakable factor of success which no person can refute.

KPIs are always a quantity which both an employee and the manager or partner can agree to accomplish, providing an ultimate measurement for evaluation and appraisal of performance.

Kibitzer

A Yiddish term that implies an individual in a company or firm who looks on and offers unwanted and usually meddlesome advice to the team.

Kibitzers normally are not members of the team with which they kibitz, but when they are members the Team Leader must take corrective action at the beginning of the team's project to insure that the Kibitzer changes into a productive member or is dismissed from the team.

L

Leader, Business

In business, a person who leads or guides others in achieving the objective or the mission, and who is in charge or command of others.

One cannot train a person to become a great leader, no matter how much academia says to the contrary, because the highest degree of leadership occurs naturally in a Business Leader.

Leader, Management

A partner or manager who is proficient in management work as opposed to specialist work, utilizing the six functions of management in working through and with people to achieve objectives: Strategy, Planning, Organizing, Leading, Teamwork, and Control.

In management, a leader does not have to be a manager; but a manager must be a leader. During the progression of a manager, leadership traits go from being a doer-manager to a delegator-manager to achieve objectives.

Leader, Team (See Team Leader)

Leadership

A manager or partner who has the capacity to lead others in accomplishing objectives with metrics.

The best leaders are normally the best specialists but not

necessarily the best managers. Leadership is the quality that allows others to remain motivated to accomplish the objectives due to the style of the partner or manager themselves.

Leadership Attributes

A quality or characteristic of a leader which when combined with the activities of the six functions of management, produce the characteristics of a great leadership manager.

Attributes include the following and more: humility, humanity, courage, accountable, knowledge, communication, commitment, see trends, sense of humor, creativity, innovation, visionary, compassionate, positive attitude, analytical, empathy, drive, confidence, smart, intelligent, respected, authoritative, honesty, integrity, enthusiastic, delegator, decisive, decision maker, organizer, trust, developer of people, and others.

Leadership Management

A style of management where a manager or partner implements the six functions of management to achieve objectives, with heavier emphasis on the activities of leading than the activities of the other functions of management, in particular strong communications, accountability, decision making, action planning and utilizing metrics.

Leadership is a function of management that every manager and partner must implement, but those managers and partners who focus more on logical decision making and two-way communications are considered leadership managers.

Leadership Management, Stages of

The level of Leadership that is required within the four stages of a Manager: First Line or Supervisory; Middle

Management; Executive Management; and General Management.

The more that an individual manager or partner progresses within a company or firm, the more leadership is required to motivate the larger organization that he is managing. This explains one reason why managers and partners do not progress to the higher levels of management at the executive level.

Leadership Style

The demeanor and approach to objectives and metrics that a manager or partner professes with their direct reports so that the mission is accomplished.

The normal style of a first line manager is that of a Doer Manager, one who is the expert specialist but not expert in the six (6) functions of management. The middle manager remains a Doer Manager but is progressing into working through and with others. The executive manager has mastered the techniques of the 21st Century in delegation and accountability, working almost completely through and with others to achieve objectives. The general manager works completely through and with others. (See Manager, Doer; Manager, Delegator)

Leading

Is one of the Six Functions of Management, and is defined as showing the way or guiding your direct reports by going in advance of others. It is characterized by achieving objectives with metrics through a team effort, through and with others.

One cannot train a manager or partner to be leading others, it is a natural phenomenon of being a solid manager or partner that you automatically lead in advance of others, and you are the first to stand when asked for a volunteer. (See Function of Management, Leading)

Level, Manager

A Manager who has developed into one of the four stages of a Manager: First Line or Supervisory; Middle Management; Executive Management; and General Management.

It is important to understand that there is accountability at every level of management in a firm or company. In order to determine which individual in a company or firm is the accountable person for a specific piece of work, a manager or partner must trace the line of authority. (See Accountability, Requirements for; Tracing the Line of Authority)

Line Correlation

The line relationship that a partner or manager has in being fully accountable for accomplishing a key objective of the firm or company.

The individual could be a staff or line partner or manager in having such a Line Correlation for achieving an objective. (See Relationship, Line; Relationship, Staff)

Line of Authority

In management, the Line of Authority is a series of points or dots, as in geometry, which identifies the individual having the authority for a particular work or responsibility.

In accountability, the function of authority is one of the three ingredients required to have accountability for any work at any level of the organization. By "tracing the line of authority" for a particular work or responsibility, the partner or manager is able to know exactly who is accountable for that work or responsibility. (See Tracing the Line of Authority)

Logic Gap

A break in the core process of management, where the gap restricts or prohibits the accomplishment of an objective with metrics. This could be any step in the management process from establishing the mission, to drilling-down the objectives and metrics to every level of the organization; to having an appropriate performance evaluation & appraisal process.

Logic Gaps in a management process are best seen by the workers themselves, and reflect negatively upon management because of the decrease in productivity and efficiency that occurs because of the gaps. For example, whenever a manager or partner establishes objectives without metrics, the organization begins work without knowing what will measure the accomplishment of the objective. That is a logic gap in a process of management.

In this emerging real-time business environment, size is no longer a decisive advantage. Speed and agility win the moment.

David Meerman Scott
The New Rules of Marketing & PR

Vocabulary & Axioms for Professional Managers and Partners
2nd Edition © Gregory N. Weismantel, 2014

Management Attitude or Disposition

The sum of traits that identify a manager or partner who achieves objectives through his own experience and expertise, or achieves objectives through and with a team of individuals.

Management Attitude or Disposition will either bring down a manager or partner over the long term, or will lead them to overwhelming success within an organization because of the number of objectives achieved.

Management Authority

The ability or official capacity of a manager or partner to exercise total control over the actions of any direct report in any responsibility or work.

Management Authority is always associated with managerial power within an organization, and is always driven from a higher level to a lower level. In a management process, the "line of authority" determines who is accountable for a particular type of work, and "tracing the line of authority" always identifies who is accountable for that work.

Management by Objectives (MBO)

A process popularized by the late Peter Drucker in the late 1950's which professed the theory that managers and employees each set their own list of objectives and then set out through the year to accomplish them.

MBO was not a viable management process because it lacked a metric as the goal of the objective setting process, and therefore during the annual period of employee evaluation & appraisal, the employee and the manager could never agree on the actual accomplishment of the objectives, since there were no measurements agreed to. This was a perfect example where an individual who had no significant management experience became the guru of theory for managers in business.

Management Depth

The management depth of a company or firm relates to the number of individuals, managers or partners who have developed the managerial skill sets of management work to achieve objectives through and with others, and are the "next man in" for positions of increased accountability. (See Leadership Management)

The skill sets for management depth are found in all the activities of the functions of leadership management, with particular emphasis on those activities of accountability, decision making, communicating, action planning, and utilizing metrics in managing.

Management Development

The process by which a manager or partner enrich themselves through studying the concepts and axioms of management in conjunction with the six functions of management and their activities.

Management Development is not a company or firm accountability per se, because it involves 90% individual work and 10% company work, whereas Management Training involves 90% company work and 10% individual work. It is the line managers and partners who are accountable for development of their lower level managers and potential partners. (See Development, Manager)

Management Process

A system of operations and actions in the management of a company or firm based upon accountability, that bring about harmonious teamwork between Executive Managers and Partners, Middle Managers, and First Line Managers and their corresponding direct reports.

Effective Management Processes begin with tracing the line of authority and thereby defining the accountability that each individual in the organization has with each level of management.

Management Tenet

A doctrine or axiom that has been proven to be true and held as being definite based upon use by partners and managers regarding a set of principles, functions and relationships of the process of management. (See Axiom)

Management tenets are critical processes that have been proven by actual managers and partners over a period of years, and not a part of unproven theory developed by academia.

Management Training

The process of training a manager or partner in the techniques which can be utilized within an organization with their direct reports. Examples of such techniques are decision making and problem solving, as well as techniques for developing and managing teams.

Management Training is 90% company work and 10% individual work. These techniques can be trained, but the likelihood of utilization increases with the number of truly professional managers which develop the techniques with their direct reports. (See Management Tenet)

Management Work

The work that managers and partners perform in the six

functions of management, and their corresponding segments of activities: Strategy, Planning, Organizing, Leading, Teamwork, and Control.

The most difficult of work is Management Work, because of his or her accountability for the key objectives of the mission. (Also see Specialist Work; Work, Management; Work, Specialist)

Management, Assumptive

A management style which is characterized by assumption of objectives being cascaded or drilled-down to lower levels of the organization, and where metrics are taken for granted, without any basis of accountability.

Traits of assumptive management are reflected in the product/services quadrant in which the company's products and services reside, and they are usually all in the aging quadrant. In a company where Assumptive Management is involved there is little or no management work (i.e., use of the six functions of management) within their management process.   The product quadrants are the best indicator that this is occurring, with few growth products or services found in the process of establishing Strategy within the company or firm.   Strategy is one of the six functions of management.

Management, Operations

The category of management which is the process of identifying "how the organization will achieve its mission, and what actions it will take to get there, both strategically and operationally."

Operations management occurs on an annual basis, with ongoing annual objectives renewed each year for success. A company or firm can be very successful only utilizing Operations Management on an annual basis. (Also see Management, Strategic)

Management, Science of

The observation, identification, description, and explanation of best practice management techniques of successful firms and companies in which managers and partners are required to study and practice in order to be successful.

The science of management provides AXIOMs and techniques for managing successful firms and companies.

Management, Strategic

The category of management which is the process of identifying the vision and reality as to "<u>what the organization should be</u>" regarding what is driving the success of the company, the driving force.

Strategic Management is only beneficial if the organization has a high degree of efficiency in its Operations Management. It is observed that those companies who utilize Strategic Management in conjunction with Operations Management are the most successful companies. (Also See Management, Operations)

Manager

Is a person who is in charge of a business or a portion thereof; who directs, controls, and supervises the resources of that business, and the accomplishment of its mission.

Notice in this definition that there is no requirement that a manager have people reporting to him.

Manager Vs. Leader

The difference between a Manager and a Leader is determined by the fact that a Leader achieves objectives utilizing leadership capabilities alone; while a Manager achieves objectives through and with others by utilizing all six functions of management which includes leadership.

In business, a manager must be a leader; but a leader does not necessarily have to be a manager. The same can be said of a partner of a firm. The manner in which a professional manager or partner approaches problems through and with the team is a profound difference between the two.

Manager, Delegator (Partner)

Is a Manager or Partner who achieves objectives by using the innate ability and specialist knowledge <u>of the team</u> and delegates the proper authority to team members so that they accomplish his objectives without his decision making.

A Delegator Manager is a professional manager or partner who utilizes the resources of the organization to achieve objectives by delegating the objective and the authority to accomplish that objective to lower levels, and delegating with metrics. (See Empowerment)

Manager, Doer (Partner)

Is a Manager or Partner who achieves objectives by using his own innate ability as well as the specialist knowledge of the work involved, with little reliance upon metrics as measurements.

A Doer Manager or Partner is one whose style is normally that of a first line manager or supervisor and a middle manager because it is at this entry level where an individual's achievements transition from achieving objectives by themselves to achieving objectives through and with others. (See Manager, Professional)

Manager, Executive (Partner)

The third level of a partner or manager's career occurs with the progression through middle management to the director and vice president or partner level. At this stage the partner or Executive Manager has become a delegator manager and is considered a professional manager.

At the Partner or Executive Manager level the objectives are achieved working with others and the amount of management work far outnumbers the amount of specialist work that the Partner or Executive Manager performs.

Manager, First Line

The first level of a partner or manager's career begins with his or her becoming a First Line Manager or Supervisor. He normally is promoted to manager because he was the best worker on the widget line, so he was placed in control to supervise the workers of all the widget machines.

A First Line Manager or Supervisor has the traits of a Doer Manager, and not a Delegator Manager. (See Manager, Doer; Manager, Delegator)

Manager, General

The fourth level of a partner or manager's career occurs after working as an Executive Manager or Partner over several years of service, and exemplifying a strong degree of advanced management techniques using management tenets and logical decision making.

The General Manager is normally the CEO accountable to the Board of Directors of the company, or is the Managing Partner of a firm or Partnership accountable to the Executive Board of Partners of the firm. His or her objectives are professionally achieved with metrics, working through the executive team, and he or she is always accountable to the board for achieving the mission of the company or firm.

Manager, Line (or Partner)

A Line Manager is any manager or partner of the company or firm who is accountable for achieving the key objectives and metrics which are driven by the mission.

A Line Manager or Partner requires complete support from the staff managers or partners in order to be totally successful in achieving the key objectives. An example of a line unit in the military would be those units which win the battles, and the war, and are predominantly the infantry, artillery, and tank units of the operation. Staff units would be those units which support the line, such as supplies of petrol, ammunition, food, bridge building (engineers), and maintenance units. Which are the most important, line or staff units?

Manager, Middle

The second level of a partner or manager's career occurs when a first line manager has proven that he or she can manage more responsibility than what they managed as a first line manager.

The Middle Manager maintains the traits of a Doer Manager, and not a Delegator Manager, but progression to successful managing through and with others begins at this stage, and toward becoming a professional manager or partner.

Manager, Professional (or Partner)

A Professional Manager or Partner is one who achieves objectives with metrics while working with a team of individuals, allowing the team to manage themselves based on delegating the objectives with the function of Control (metrics).

In the 21st Century it is a necessity to understand how to delegate objectives with metrics, and establish a new line of authority throughout the organization. Professional Partners and Managers master that technique and are successful with their firms and companies because they achieve their objectives through and with others.

Manager, Staff (or Partner)

A Staff Manager or Staff Partner is any manager or partner of the company or firm who is NOT accountable for achieving the key objectives and metrics which are driven by the mission, but is accountable for fully supporting the line managers and partners in any manner in which they require support and service.

From experience, the most successful companies are those with the best Staff Managers, not the best Line Managers. A company or firm can be very successful with a mediocre Line Management group and a top-notch Staff Management group, but less successful with a top Line Management group and a mediocre Staff Management group.

Measurable Objectives

The technique of utilizing metrics to measure the accomplishment of an objective.

This is a major tenet of management, and all professional managers utilize metrics to manage their teams and departments for the objectives they determine will achieve the mission of the organization.

Measure

In the process of evaluation, the individual employee measures herself for the accomplishment of objectives to agreed-upon metrics. This is called self-evaluation.

This process is for those managers who want to be the Professional Managers of the 21st Century, and who master the utilization of metrics in management.

Mentor, Management

In business, a wise and trusted counselor and expert in the functions and techniques of management.

Mentors are those former managers and partners who can relate to the actual undertaking and decisions that another manager or partner must undertake, and does not profess any theoretical concepts only actual ones learned from being a manager or partner. A manager or partner must be careful as to whom the proper mentor should be to aid in the area of management, as too many academia espouse theory and not the blocking & tackling. (See Work, Management)

Mentor, Specialist

In business, a wise and trusted counselor and expert in the specialist work of the company or firm.

(See Mentor, Management; Work, Specialist)

Metric

A rule or test on which a judgment or decision can be based, which measures the accomplishment of an objective.

Without the use of a metric, accomplishment of an objective becomes an arbitrary condition that produces conflict between a manager or partner and his or her subordinates. With a metric for the objective, that is agreed-to by both the manager or partner and the subordinate, there can be little doubt whether the objective is accomplished or not. The metric is the protection which Professional Managers and Partners use to avoid personal conflict in the 21st Century.

Metric, Qualitative

A measurement of the accomplishment of an objective which does not have a quantifiable definition such as a Key

Performance Indicator (KPI), but reflects the qualitative performance in a subjective manner.

Qualitative Metrics (Yes or No measurements) should be utilized to measure objectives when no exact quantitative measurement is available, but as seldom as possible. Utilizing Qualitative Metrics as a partner or manager will normally promote disagreement and dissension between the manager or partner and their subordinates in accomplishing objectives. (See Key Performance Indicator, KPI; also see Goal)

Metric, Quantitative

A measurement of the accomplishment of an objective which has a numerical definition, such as a key performance indicator (KPI), and reflects a distinct level of performance that is expected to achieve an objective in a precise manner.

The rule of thumb for a professional manager or partner in the 21st Century is to utilize Quantitative Metrics with all objectives that are drilled-down to other direct reports in your organization, and receive agreement and understanding of the metric so that objectives can be achieved by the individual reporting to the partner or manager. Quantitative Metrics allow the individuals to evaluate themselves, not the manager or partner, whose role now is to appraise how the subordinate achieved the objective not if they achieved it. (See Key Performance Indicator, KPI; Drill Down of Objectives; Evaluation, Self)

Metrics, Development of

In operational management, the process in which a direct report of a manager or partner prepares the measurements which they determine are appropriate for the responsibility or work for which the direct report is accountable.

Objective setting is an activity of the planning function of management; developing metrics is an activity of the control function of management. Note that in operational management the process for the Development of Metrics begins with the direct report, and goes up to the manager for agreement. (See Performance Metrics, Development of)

Mission

An activity of the Strategy function of management. The Mission is the company or firm's reason for being.

In strategy, the Mission is a brief statement that expresses the firm's current and future reason for being but is not considered to be the operational statement that is developed with the operational plans of the company or firm, called the mission statement.

Mission Statement

An activity of the Planning function of management. The Mission Statement is driven from the mission of strategy, but includes all the commitments that the CEO or Managing Partner make to the customer, products and services, financial, and people.

The Mission Statement is what drives the key objectives and metrics of the CEO or Managing Partner, which is why the statement should include the commitments shown.

Motivation

In a management process, Motivation is the process of using certain techniques to provide the incentive or motive for an employee to take action according to agreed-upon metrics to achieve an objective.

When discussing motivation with a partner or manager it is not only important to discuss what motivates the partner or manager's direct reports, but also what motivates the motivator. Motivation is a segment of activity of the Leading function of management.

Motivation, Compelling

The action of a manager or partner to motivate a direct report by pressure or force of word or action to complete the objective.

In today's politically correct world, compelling an employee to do something is not nearly as frequent as it was in days past, but even today it is a type of motivation that we see from doer managers, and of course in the military service, where commands are obeyed by rote. Motivation is a segment of activity of the Leading function of management. (See Motivation, Impelling)

Motivation, Encouragement

The action of a manager or partner to motivate a direct report by inspiring with complete confidence to achieve the objective.

Encouragement Motivation is one of the best ways to motivate employees, but must be accompanied with realistic objectives and metrics. Motivation is a segment of activity of the Leading function of management. (See, Axiom of the Realistic Metric)

Motivation, Impelling

The action of a manager or partner to motivate a direct report by urging to action through moral pressure to complete the objective.

Impelling Motivation is useful when a company or firm wishes to impress on their sustainability methods. Motivation is a segment of activity of the Leading function of Management.

Motivation, Incentive or Money

The action of a manager or partner to motivate a direct report by providing a monetary incentive to complete the objective.

The use of money as a motivator is only a short term motivational tool for the manager or partner. Once you provide the monetary incentive to complete the objective that he or she is already accountable for, the individual then expects this to occur ongoing, even to the point where the individual plans on the incentive is a part of his or her salary. Money is known to have a very short term period of motivation. Motivation is a segment of activity of the Leading function of management.

Motivation, Inspiring

The action of a manager to motivate a direct report by stimulating the emotions and intellect to a high level of creativity to complete the objective.

Inspiring a team or department is an important way for a manager to achieve results. One drawback is that it does not work consistently unless the objectives are consistently achieved, which is why the metric (control) is such an important ingredient to achieving objectives with a team of partners or managers, from top to lower levels. Motivation is a segment of activity of the Leading function of management.

Motivation, Using Bonus for

The action of a manager or partner to use money, goods, or services provided by management in excess of what is normally received in salary or wages, for those individuals who have provided an inordinate amount of work or success in the company achieving its annual objectives.

A bonus utilizing money, goods or services as a motivator has a very short term motivational period that often becomes expected regardless of the amount of inordinate work achieved. Motivation is a segment of activity of the Leading function of management.

Motivation, Using Money For

The process of utilizing money to motivate individuals to achieve more ongoing objectives than what are expected to be achieved regularly.

In a management process, money should only be considered as a very short term motivator, because once money is used to motivate an organization the employees will consider it to be a part of their regular salary and wage package. Motivation is a segment of activity of the Leading function of management.

Multi-Faceted Metric

Is a metric which requires more than one Key Performance Indicator (KPI) to measure the overall accomplishment of an objective.

Utilizing a Multi-Faceted Metric should be seldom, but occasionally there is a measure that requires more than one quantitative number to determine its accomplishment.

"What makes strategic management so difficult is that it is conceived in the present, which is operational, but designed for the assumed future, which is not."

Greg Weismantel

Vocabulary & Axioms for Professional Managers and Partners
2nd Edition © Gregory N. Weismantel, 2014

Nameplate, Manager's (or Partner's)

A plate or plaque inscribed with the manager or partner's name as well as their title, as on an office door.

Management work is the hardest of work, and therefore achieving the position of the manager or partner is an important and critical achievement at the four levels of a manager in a firm or company. The use of nameplates is an important ingredient to acknowledging the achievement of a manager or partner, and both their office and attire should reflect a partner or manager's acumen and skills.

Narrative, Manager

Information included in a management process that does not function in the process itself but that is used by the manager or partner to identify and correct individual performance to achieve objectives.

Manager Narrative is often found in the sidebar notes of the manager in relation to a direct report's agreement to the metrics of the objective. This allows the manager to revert back to the direct report's understanding of the meaning of the metrics at the time the objective is agreed-to by the direct report.

Natural Decision Making (See Decision Making, Natural)

Negotiation

The process of conferring with another individual or entity of an outside source where the intent is to gain an advantage in reaching an agreement.

The intent of Negotiations with entities outside your company or firm is always to gain an advantage.

Negotiation, Management

The process of conferring with another manager or partner in order to reach an agreement on the objective and metrics of a plan.

The intent of Management Negotiations within your company is to improve the ability of the company or firm to meet its mission or objectives. The problem with management negotiation is that it often dilutes the real problem during the problem analysis of decision making, and therefore not fully resolving the total issue.

Network, Manager (or Partner)

A system of unrelated managers or partners who all study and practice the tenets of management and resemble a net in consisting of the four levels of management that cross, branch out, or interconnect usually sharing a large proportion of their managerial expertise.

Networking by managers and partners is a common undertaking, and those managers or partners who master the six functions of management and their corresponding segments and activities have the larger networks due to their demand by others. Manager networks on social media sites are one area of importance, and particularly in the social media network of LinkedIn.

Objective Evaluation

In the process of self-evaluation, an individual's determination that the metrics of an objective have been met must not be influenced by emotion, surmise, or personal prejudice and only be based on observable phenomena of the metric presented factually.

Objective Evaluation is an activity of the Control function of management, and occurs during the evaluation and appraisal of an individual's objectives and metrics in the management process.

Objective, Annual (aka Fiscal)

Time-denoted objectives which are established by a manager or partner with metrics that must be accomplished during a specific 12-month period.

Annual objectives by themselves are inadequate to manage an organization or firm to a higher degree of efficiency. The major reason for this is that annual objectives have no direct correlation with the organization's mission, nor their partner or manager's objectives, nor with the employees at lower levels.

Objective, Key

Key Objectives are those ongoing plans which stem from the commitments of the mission statement and are cascaded and drilled down through all four levels of managers to the individual employee.

In a management process, an individual will have ongoing key objectives and normally will also have time-denoted annual objectives as well. Both will be supported by measurements, metrics, which determine the accomplishment of the objectives.

Objective, Operational

An Operational Objective is any key or annual objective which relates directly to the operational plan of the organization during a time-denoted period, usually the 12-month fiscal year of the company or firm.

Successful companies and firms all have critical operational objectives with metrics within their operational management process.

Objective, Strategic

A Strategic Objective is a key objective which relates to the strategic plan of the organization during its three years of implementation and is the accountability of the executive managers and partners of the company or firm.

Strategic Objectives are only utilized by a company or firm that implements strategic management in conjunction with operational management. This means that the enterprise must have a 3-year strategic plan with strategic objectives and metrics, with the first year of the strategic plan being the current year's operational plan.

Objectives, Establishment of Annual

In a management process, Establishment of Annual Objectives is optional but such objectives are established for the purpose of achieving some annual project that will help the organization as a whole or for the development of an individual in particular.

In the process of developing a managers and partners, Annual

Objectives are used as the tool for a lower level of manager or potential partner to develop skills for the next higher managerial position.

Objectives, Establishment of Ongoing (Continuous)

In a management process for the 21st Century, Establishment of Ongoing Objectives occurs from the ongoing tasks or responsibilities found in the job description of an individual, which includes the cascaded or drilled-down portions of the work that the manager or partner above this individual has delegated to lower levels.

Ongoing Objectives, also called Continuous Objectives, will always remain with the job position itself, no matter if the individual leaves the company or firm or just that position. It is the metric to these Ongoing Objectives which will remain, based upon the individual's skill set.

Occurrence, Abnormal

In the Technique for Sound Decision Making, the Abnormal Occurrence is where the apparent problem occurs.

It is quite common to have the very first comment on what the real problem is, actually be the apparent problem or the symptom of the real problem. Managers in the 21st Century must use their time and skills productively, particularly with their departments and teams, since the resources of labor will be at a premium. (See Occurrence, Normal)

Occurrence, Normal

In the Technique for Sound Decision Making, the Normal Occurrence is compared to the Abnormal Occurrence with the delta being where the real problem rests.

Normal Occurrence is a step in the Logical Decision Making Technique when a manager or partner looks at the apparent problem versus what normally occurs. This is a key step in finding the real problem, because the team will have a coordinated action plan to resolve the real problem not the apparent problem or symptom. (See Occurrence, Abnormal)

Operational

Of or pertaining to the objectives and metrics of management for operating a business or firm for one fiscal year, in a pragmatic fashion.

Operational management is the only requirement for managing a successful company or firm. However, when operational management combines with strategic management the potential level of success doubles for most companies and firms. (See Management, Operational; Management, Strategic)

Operationalization

In leadership management, Operationalization is usually referred to in strategic initiatives when the vision of the future driving force of the company or firm differs from the current driving force, and the delta is not theoretical whatsoever, but pragmatic and heuristic. It is also measurable with metrics.

The reason for this is because leadership management achieves objectives and goals through and with others, and operationalization projects that the vision and purpose of the company or firm combine into operational teamwork that is unbeatable.

Operator

An employee of a company or firm who has the responsibility for the specialist work required to implement the products or services of a company or firm.

The Operator of a company or firm usually has the specialist skills for completely implementing the products and services and this expertise is what normally is observed as the reason to promote that individual from an Operator to a first line manager or supervisor who manages several Operators.

Order

To command an employee of a company or firm to take responsibility for a certain task or job within the operational area of the company or firm.

Orders are usually a sign of the management style of the natural leader who achieves objectives and metrics through his or her own expertise, not a professional manager who achieves objectives and metrics through and with the team or department personnel.

Organization Chart

A graphic illustration of the units of work of a company or firm, which also shows the personnel of the units who are accountable to the First Line, Middle, Executive, and General Managers (or Managing Partners) in a company or firm for the units of work.

An Organizational Chart is the basis for cascading objectives and metrics from the mission of the company or firm from the President/CEO or Managing Partner, all the way down to the lowest individual in the organization.

Organization, Business

A number of units of business having many specific accountabilities, united for a particular purpose or mission, and comprised of management levels of First Line, Middle, Executive, and General Managers.

A Business Organization can be large or small, but still have levels of management. Professional firms will also have a partner and managing partner level.

Organization, Integrated

To combine multiple units of work from disparate organizations with different missions, objectives and metrics, into a whole new organization that operates with one mission, objective and metric.

In the 21st Century, managers and partners need to know the concepts and principles behind Integrated Organizations so that they can provide the most effective and efficient organizational structure with fewer direct reports and fewer managers.

Organization, Matrix

The type of organizational structure which allows pools of highly specialist individuals to have multiple accountabilities in different projects for different project managers, while reporting to the pool manager at the same time.

A Matrix Organization is the most difficult of organizations to manage because one individual will have multiple bosses to whom he or she is accountable. The matrix organization can only be successful long term when definite authority is traced to all levels of decision making, and maintained ongoing. It also is the most productive and efficient when these accountabilities are established and understood by all members of the organization

Organization, Most Effective

The structure of the organization which has a management process that allows for most efficiency out of the managerial levels of the company or firm, while allowing the line managers or partners to achieve their key objectives and metrics in the quickest manner possible.

Line managers and partners are the only ones accountable for achieving the key objectives of the firm or company, not staff managers, so it is critical to have line managers and partners capable to achieve their objectives in a timely fashion. (See Manager, Line; Manager, Staff)

Organization, Most Efficient

The structure of the organization which has a management process that allows for the most productivity and the least amount of wasted effort out of each managerial level of the company or firm.

A combination of the Most Efficient Organization and the Most Effective Organization is what the CEO and Managing Partner strive for.

Organizational Structure

The type of structure of a company or firm, traditional or matrix.

Functional grouping of the units of work is how the type of firm is structured, and this is an activity of the Organizing function of management.

Organizational Restructuring

The process by which a manager or partner at any level of the organization will reorganize the work and the people performing the work with the objective of increasing productivity within the work force and improving efficiency in core processes.

There are two types of restructuring, each with different objectives. 1) Restructuring annually, to clean out obsolete processes and work. In this case the objective is NOT to lose one person. 2) Restructuring when the business is close to bankruptcy. In this case the objective is to lose people and cut fixed costs to breakeven.

Organizing

Is a function of management. Organizing is to arrange the work of an organization in a coherent, orderly, and structured pattern, so that it can be accomplished in the most productive manner in achieving the objective or the mission of the organization.

A manager or a partner of a company or firm should reorganize his unit of work every year, toward the end of the fiscal year, in order to maintain a high degree of efficiency within the unit as well as to analyze and update its core processes. (See Core Process)

Organizing Around the People

During the process of restructuring the organization, there is a natural tendency to place tenured managers or partners into a position when that individual does not have the management or specialist skills to perform the work required for that position.

Organizing Around the People is a cardinal sin in restructuring an organization because it nullifies the skill set required for the position in favor of an individual that might not have that skill set.

Organizing Around the Work

During the process of restructuring the organization, the first management tenet is to always organize around the work, not around the people.

Organizing Around the Work is not a difficult concept to comprehend, but always seems to be the most difficult concept to implement. Too often in the annual restructuring exercise that a CEO or Managing Partner performs, there is a subjective preference to restructure the organization based upon the current people that are employees, not upon whether the current employees are the best at the skills required for the position. Until the organization's structure is "Organized Around the Work" there will always be the need for "assistants" who have the skill sets to accomplish the work without help.

Outcome

A natural result or consequence of achieving an objective with metrics in a management process.

The result of achieving an objective is normally positive in nature, however, if the objective resolves the apparent problem and not the real problem then the outcome results in wasted effort by the team which is accountable for achieving the objective with metric, and new effort is required.

Output

The energy, power, or work produced by a company or firm, department, or team in achieving objectives with metrics in a management process.

Managers must be particularly cognizant of the amount of energy, power, and work required to achieve objectives, which is why the decision making process is so critical in determining the real problem from the apparent problem. (See Problem, Apparent; Problem, Real)

"Sometimes when you innovate you make mistakes. It is best to admit them quickly, and get on with your other innovative ideas."

Steve Jobs

Paradigm, Management

A philosophical framework of managing in which the axioms of leadership management, which have been proven by successful companies and firms, provide managers and partners the process for reacting to forces of business.

In the 21st Century there is a new paradigm for managing the social media driven companies and firms, allowing each individual the authority to take action as quickly as possible.

Performance

In a management process, the act or style of any individual performing a work or responsibility, or an objective, according to a measurement (metric) that can be quantitative or qualitative in nature.

Setting an objective is an activity of the Planning function of management; while the metric is an activity of the Control function of management. (See Metric, Qualitative; Metric, Quantitative)

Performance Appraisal

In a management process, the Performance Appraisal of an individual is "how" the individual accomplished the objectives and metrics, and is totally subjective in nature as to whether the objectives were achieved in a satisfactory or unsatisfactory manner, and not evaluating the work itself.

Performance Appraisal has nothing to do with the metric or the objective, and is strictly a subjective appraisal by the manager or partner of an individual on how they did the work. The manager or partner only appraises and corrects the manner in which the objective was accomplished. Appraisal is an activity of the Control function of management. (See Performance Evaluation)

Performance, Correcting

The process by which a manager or partner of a company or firm will improve work performance and results achieved by an individual based upon performance.

Improving Work Performance and Results Achieved is an activity of the Control function of management, and should always utilize a formal action plan with the individual to do so.

Performance Evaluation

In a management process, the evaluation of an individual based on accomplishing his or her objectives and metrics is either satisfactory performance or unsatisfactory performance and is <u>totally objective in nature</u> according to the metric of the objective.

With management in the 21st Century, managers and partners should not be accountable to evaluate performance of their direct reports. By utilizing agreed-to metrics and KPIs, all employees should evaluate themselves. Evaluation is an activity of the Control function of management. Whereas Performance Evaluation is objective, Performance Appraisal is subjective. (See Performance Appraisal)

Performance Evaluation, Satisfactory

Performance Evaluation is always objective related to the metric (i.e., it is met or not met), so that Satisfactory Performance is always the condition when metrics are met by the individual or manager.

Managers and partners in the 21st Century will delegate proper authority with metrics to lower levels of the organization so that each individual including the manager and partner can objectively evaluate themselves according to agreed-to metrics. Evaluation is an activity of the Control function of management.

Performance Evaluation, Unsatisfactory

In a Management Process, the Evaluation and Appraisal of an individual based on accomplishing their objectives and metrics is either Satisfactory Performance or Unsatisfactory. The evaluation is always objective related to the metric, it is met or not met, so that Unsatisfactory Performance is always denoted when metrics are not met by the individual.

Managers and partners in the 21st Century will delegate proper authority with metrics to lower levels of the organization, allowing each individual to evaluate themselves according to a metric. Evaluation is an activity of the Control function of management.

Performance Metrics

Specific measurements which relate to the actual type of achievement of strategic objectives that an executive manager or partner wants to see from a team leader or other key manager or partner reporting to him. These include specific Key Performance Indicators (KPI) which are more precise than normal.

Performance Metrics are normally found in strategic management, where the strategic action plans of the strategy are the accountability of key executives of the company, or key partners of the firm. (See Strategic Management)

Performance Metrics, Development of

In Strategic Management, the process in which a CEO of a company or a Managing Partner of a firm prepares the measurements which she determines are appropriate for achieving the Strategic Action Plans, which are the accountability of the key Vice Presidents or Partners.

Note that in strategic management, the process for the Development of Performance Metrics begins with the top manager of the company or firm, and goes down to the key vice presidents and key partners for execution. This is the opposite of developing metrics in Operational Management, where the lower levels are involved in developing the metrics. (See Metrics, Development of)

Performance Review

A retrospective view of the current and past performance of a manager, partner, department or individual employee of a company or firm which can occur annually or upon the request of a manager or partner.

Performance Reviews are normally used as the basis for annual or periodic increases in compensation, salary and wages, or benefits for annual/fiscal year performance. They also can occur by exception when an individual has achieved a milestone of accomplishment during the fiscal year, and has pre-arranged to receive a compensation increase when milestones are met. Managers and partners should be aware of the ramifications of motivating with money, as it has a very short time span. (See Motivation, Using Money for; Motivation, Using Bonus for)

Persona, Company or Firm

In developing strategy, the persona is the image of how a company or firm is observed outwardly by other individuals, companies or firms as distinguished from the internal representation of what you are.

The persona of a customer is important because when observed by your company or firm it allows your R&D department to have a series of criteria to develop new products for the emerging quadrant that appeal to the customer. In analyzing the persona of a company or firm it should include their Needs, Competition, Image, Products & Services, Markets they sell in, and their Problems. This same scenario should be analyzed for your own company or firm to insure it matches with the products and services you are offering to your customers or clients.

Plan

A detailed scheme, program, or method worked out beforehand for the accomplishment of an objective utilizing a systematic arrangement of details.

While a scheme might sound devious, it is appropriate for a manager or partner to scheme for the good of the company or firm in accomplishing the mission. (See Planning)

Planning

To formulate a scheme or program for the accomplishment or attainment of a manager or partner's objectives, or the mission of the organization.

Planning is an area which most managers prefer the most. The reason is simple: it is their plans with which they are working. It is also an area where the direct reports of a partner or manager differ on how well they plan. When direct reports are included in the planning process, the manager or partner is viewed as a manager-delegator and commitment by the direct reports normally occurs.

Plans, Action

A formal, written, time-denoted plan which reflects an action required during a specific period of time to achieve an objective during that specific time, with accountability established for each step of the plan by the participants.

Action Plans are not "to do" lists, and should only be utilized as a formal, written plan when a problem is being resolved by several individuals, departments or teams.

Plans, Action, Strategic

Formal, written time-denoted plans with metrics, which reflect an action required during a specific fiscal year to achieve a strategic objective during that fiscal year, and are the accountability of the executives of the company or firm.

Strategic Action Plans are the accountability of the key executives of the company or key partners of the firm, as these individuals are the managers normally accountable for maneuvering the company through its growth cycle.

Plans, Fiscal Year

Formal, written, time-denoted plans which reflect objectives and metrics which must be accomplished within the fiscal year of an organization so that the mission is accomplished.

Fiscal Year plans are also known as operation plans, and most companies only utilize Fiscal Year Plans to manage their business. When a company or firm has a 3-year strategic plan or 3-year strategic initiative, the first year is the Fiscal Year plan, and is operational in nature; the remaining two years are strategic.

Plans, Individual Ongoing

Formal, written, continuous plans which reflect the ongoing objectives and metrics of the individual for managing a business, department, or his own accountabilities.

At no time should an individual reporting to a manager or partner have more than three Individual Ongoing Plans with metrics. Always use the 20-80 Rule for determining the critical objectives which must be accomplished by the individual, and use the management function of Control (metrics) to measure performance ongoing

Plans, Long Range

Are informal plans that do not have any accountability for accomplishment by managers of a company or partners of a firm, and only reflect the dreams of the visionaries of the company or firm, and not the strategic or operational management.

Long range plans are a misnomer, but are fun to dream about during a vacation. Long Range Plans are normally developed by a Long Range Planning Committee, and it is important to remember that committees have no authority to implement the plans, only to recommend their work plans to be authorized and implemented by the CEO or Managing Partner of the organization. A planning committee has a staff relationship with the CEO or Managing Partner, which have the line relationships for that accountability.

Plans, Ongoing or Continuous

Those detailed schemes or programs which continue across time limits and are revised but never end until the operation is terminated.

Ongoing or Continuous plans are the most critical of any enterprise, company or firm, and are the accountability of each individual level of the company or firm. It is the Ongoing or Continuous Plans that require solid metrics agreed-to with the manager or partner accountable for the work delegated to lower levels, that show that an individual at any level in the company or firm is doing a good job, or not. (See Plans, Individual Ongoing)

Plans, Operational

Formal, written, time-denoted plans which reflect the short-term strategy of the operations of the company or firm.

The Operational Plans of the company or firm are usually established at least 3-months prior to the fiscal year, with objectives and metrics. When a company or firm has a 3-year Strategic Plan, the first year of the strategic plan is the Operational Plan.

Plans, Project

Formal, written time-denoted plans, which reflect all the actions required during the specified dates for accomplishing the project objectives of the project manager.

Project plans can cross fiscal year periods, but must have an opening and closing date for each fiscal year that the project generates revenue and has expenses.

Plans, Strategic

Formal, written, continuous plans which reflect the ongoing strategic objectives and metrics for the accomplishment of the mission of the company or firm for a 3-year period.

Strategic Plans are an activity of the Planning function of management, whereas developing the strategy is a function of the Strategy function of management. Strategic Plans are the direct accountability of the CEO of the company or Managing Partner of a firm. A company or firm may be successful with only implementing operational plans alone, but in combination with Strategic Planning the degree of success is magnified significantly. The most successful companies or firms in the 21st Century will all have formal Strategic Plans linked to their operational plans. (See, AXIOM of Business Strategy)

Plans, Time-Denoted

Those detailed schemes or programs which do not continue across time limits, and which have definite times denoted for accomplishment of the objectives.

Time-denoted plans must be renewed and revised following the termination of the plan due to expanding beyond the denoted time limit.   Examples of Time Denoted Plans are Action Plans, Operational Plans, and Project Plans, all with a start and stop date.

Pockets of Work

Within the Organizing function of management, by analyzing and structuring the specialist type of work required by a department or individual, Pockets of Work evolve so that the most efficient organizational structure can be achieved by individuals with the appropriate skill sets.

Pockets of Work are utilized when a manager organizes around the work, not around the people. (See, Specialist Work; Organizing Around the Work)

Policy, Company or Firm

A plan or course of action formalized by the management team of a company or firm, designed to influence and determine decisions, actions, and other matters considered to be expedient, prudent or advantageous to the company or firm.

A Policy is an activity of the Planning function of management, and combines with activities of the Leading function of management, particularly in communications.   A manager or partner should be aware that policies, like procedures, become obsolete over time, so that there should only be policies which are implemented to accommodate long term situations.   All policies should be reviewed on an annual basis to be revised or eliminated.

Position

The responsible work in which a manager or direct report of a manager is accountable for satisfactory performance based upon agreed-to measurements (metrics) with a higher level of authority in the company or firm.

Ongoing objectives for a Position do not change with the exit of the particular manager or employee, but the measurements (metrics) may change appropriately to the replacing manager's skill sets.

Position Description (See Job Description)

Position, Manager

The responsible work performed by a direct report who is a manger of the company or firm.

Manager positions belong to those individuals of the company or firm who are directly accountable for implementing the six functions of management (See Functions of Management; Delineation of Managers).

Position, Specialist

The responsible work performed by a direct report who is a non-manager of the company or firm.

Specialist positions belong to the workers of the organization who are accountable for developing and servicing the products and services of the company or firm.

Power

The ability or official capacity of a manager or partner to exercise control through authority over another manager or partner, or direct report, of the company or firm.

Power originates from the line of authority that emanates directly from a higher authority to a lower, and can be usurped without a formal leadership management process which allows the responsibilities with authority to cascade or be drilled-down to lower levels. This is the reason for the term "drill-down" of objectives and metrics. (See, Cascading of Objectives)

Power Structure

Is the tracing of the line of authority from the top level of the company or firm to the lowest level of decision making, so that there is accountability for every responsible work according to agreed-to metrics.

Without a Power Structure in a company or firm, there can be a usurping of accountable duties by managers and partners.

Powerless

Where a manager or a partner does not have the authority to make a decision for a particular work or responsibility in a company or firm.

In this case, the manager or partner can be "responsible" for accomplishing the work, but cannot be "accountable" for any decisions made about the work. (See, Assumed Authority)

Prescient Manager (Partner)

A manager or partner who has mastered the tenets of management, and through this knowledge of management actions or events the manager or partner has a distinct foresight of events before they occur.

A Prescient Manager or Prescient Partner is not a guru or does not have mysterious powers. This individual has an advantage over non-prescient managers and partners because of his or her tenacity in mastering the functions of management and their segments of activities. For example, utilizing metrics in measuring the accomplishment of the objective is commonplace with the Prescient Manager and Partner, who fully recognizes that an objective without a metric will have the same results as

Management By Objective. (See Management by Objectives, MBO)

Present Alternatives

In teamwork, individuals are motivated to present alternatives for taking action, the use of which may be approved or declined by the team or team leader.

Presenting alternatives is always considered a staff role, for supporting and servicing the team leader or manager of the team.

Price Elasticity

In creating strategy, the significance of changing the price for products and services of a company or firm has an impact on the demand for these products and services. Price elasticity occurs with all products and services that are located in the maturing quadrant of their life cycle.

Price elasticity of products and services will become less prevalent as they move into the aging quadrant of their life cycle, primarily because the competition is withdrawing from the marketplace.

Problem

A situation in operational management that presents uncertainty, or difficulty in achieving objectives or the mission of the company or firm, and which is resolved by the managers or partners of the company or firm during the core management process of decision making and problem solving.

Resolution of a Problem is the accountability of the management of the company or firm, and is often delegated down to lower levels where the Problem occurs on a consistent basis, with workers familiar with the specialist work of the problem being critical to its resolution.

Problem Analysis

Is the technique used by a partner of manager for making "sound" team decisions in logical decision making.

The key to sound decision making by a manager or partner is to differentiate the apparent problem from the real problem. The first announcement of a problem is always the apparent problem. A professional manager or partner should always solve the real problem, not a symptom of the real problem, because wasted effort by the team occurs whenever they begin work on the wrong issue or problem. (See, Problem, Real; Problem, Apparent; and Wasted Effort)

Problem Solving

Is the art of using the conclusion reached in decision making in order to achieve an objective.

The technique for sound decision making comes first, and then solving the problem through use of an action plan with metrics is the final action required of a professional partner and manager in the 21st Century era.

Problem, Apparent

In the activity of decision making, the process always starts with an analysis of the symptoms of the problem prior to gathering more facts, and this is called the Apparent Problem.

Whenever a manager or partner has his team or department taking action on an Apparent Problem, they will only resolve the symptom and not what completely resolves the problem for the company or firm. (See, Wasted Effort)

Problem, Real

In the activity of decision making, the process of gathering facts about the Apparent Problem and identifying the issues which will allow the organization to achieve objectives or the mission of the company or firm.

Resolving the Real Problem allows the department or organization to work in the most efficient manner without rework. Resolving the Apparent Problem means that the organization must then change tactics to solve the real problem, and this forces the team working on the problem to stop its current process and begin a whole different process of work. (See, Wasted Effort)

Procedure, Business

A series of steps in a course of action which is a formal method for conducting a particular work or responsibility.

A Procedure is an activity of the Planning Function of Management, and combines with activities of the Leading Function of management, particularly in communications. A manager should be aware that procedures, like policies, become obsolete over time as new processes, technology, and equipment are introduced to the organization. All procedures should be reviewed on an annual basis to be revised or completely eliminated.

Procedures, Problems with

The communication by a manager or partner of the improper series of steps in a procedure which makes the workers of the procedure to be inefficient and ineffective in achieving their objectives.

Since some manager of the company or firm is accountable for the implementation of a procedure, whenever a procedure on a wall becomes obsolete over time, the direct reports have to memorize a virtual procedure, and this promotes wasted effort within the team or department. Beware of procedures fixed in stone.

Process, Management

A system of operations of AXIOMs and the six functions of management (Strategy, Planning, Organizing, Leading, Teamwork, and Control) and the segments of activities of which are interrelated, interacting, and interdependent in achieving the mission of the company or firm.

While management involves working through and with people, it is a curve, a derivative, which is highly unpredictable because it involves people. A Management Process is linear like a road map, which a manager or partner can always refer to when she needs help, and which aids the manager in always being able to predict where you are in the process.

Process, Operational

Any process that is utilized by a company or firm, at any level of the organization, which accomplishes the mission and key objectives of the company, department, or individual.

Operational processes are always utilized with the operational plans for the fiscal year in which the objectives and metrics relate, and in most instances they are the core processes for that company, firm, or department. (See, Core Process)

Professional Manager (Partner)

A manager or partner who has mastered all the activities of the six functions of management, and consistently achieves multiple objectives by working through and with others in the company or firm.

Note that a professional partner or manager has line accountability but once they delegate the work and authority to their direct reports their functional accountability changes to staff accountability to support and serve all of their direct reports.

Profit

The return received on a business undertaking after all income revenues have been recognized legally and all operating expenses of the budgets have been met actually.

In a management process the accountability for income and profit revenues rest entirely with line units of the operation, while the accountability for operating expense budgets rests with both line and staff units of the operation. For example, the sales department is usually a line unit accountable for income revenue, but also has expense budgetary accountability associated with sales expenses at the same time. However, the administrative department does not have accountability for the income revenue of the operation, and is considered to be a staff unit, but does have the accountability for operating expense budgets.

Profit Center

The line department that is accountable for the profitable return on a business undertaking.

Profit Centers in many firms and companies represent the line departments that are accountable for the return or profit of the company or firm. Normally it is the sales or marketing departments that are the Profit Centers of a company because sales or marketing is always accountable for income revenue and contribution margin. However, it is common in organizations that are marketing driven to have the VP of Marketing and the Product Managers accountable for the profits of the organization, while the Sales Managers are accountable for the revenue generated by selling units of products or services. In manufacturing companies it could be the Business Unit Manager, or even a Plant Manager, who is accountable as the Profit Center.

Profit Formula

For a firm or company, the calculation which includes total revenue from income, minus total actual budgetary expenses to equal total profit.

Various levels of an organization could have different calculations to come up with revenue and expenses, but the total of all levels always includes the profit formula of "Revenues minus Expenses to equal Profits."

Profit Sharing

A process by which individuals, usually managers and partners, receive a share of the profits of a firm or company.

Whenever a firm or company sets up a Profit Sharing process with its partners or employees, the need to establish metrics by individual employee utilizing the Control function of management, KPI and metrics, is essential for the success of such a process. The process of evaluation and appraisal is critical for proper distribution of profits within a firm or company.

Program

An organized list of plans with objectives and metrics, including collection of data, processing, and presentation of results in a sequence of steps for which an Executive Manager is normally accountable, called a Program Manager.

Consider a Program to be similar to a project, which has multiple action plans required to complete the program, with a Program Manager accountable for all Program Action Plans in total.

Program Plans

The action plans which a program manager is accountable to accomplish.

Authority for accomplishing the Program Plans comes from a higher authority in the company or firm.

Proliferation, Negative

The process by which a negative comment or decision, either real or presumed, grows at a rapid pace throughout the company or firm.

In communication, the manager or partner at any level is accountable to make a precise decision to inform his direct reports as quickly as possible of any comment or decision which impacts the objectives of the organization. This is an activity of the Leading function of management. Negative Proliferation is most common during the activity of restructuring, which is an activity of the Organizing function of management. It also illustrates how the activities of two functions of management always operate together. (See Proliferation, Positive)

Proliferation, Positive

The process by which a positive comment or decision, either real or presumed, grows at a rapid pace throughout the company or firm.

In communication, the manager or partner at any level is accountable to make a precise decision to inform his direct reports as quickly as possible of any comment or decision which impacts the objectives of the organization. This is an activity of the Leading function of management. While Positive Proliferation appears good on the surface, it can be as devastating as Negative Proliferation when certain segments of a business hear the communication before other segments, which is why a manager or partner must be decisive in decision making while being very punctual in communicating the decision to his or her team.

Proposal

A recommended course of action for a manager, partner, or higher level of management, put forward for consideration, discussion, or adoption by a direct report, who does not have the authority to implement the course of action.

Proposals should be written, and include the following format: Purpose, Background Facts, Conclusion, and Recommendation. Recognize that proposals take a lot of effort, time and work, and if the individual proposing this course of action does not have the authority to take action then the frustration of zero action by management will be a depressing impact on further activity by the individual(s). (See, Committee)

Proposition

A statement that a manager or partner utilizes which contains predefined metrics for the critical few elements that must be accomplished in order for the statement to be justified and accepted by a higher authority.

The use of Propositions is critically important for a partner or manager to master as he or she grows from a first line supervisor, to a middle manager, to an executive manager, and then to the CEO or Managing Partner position itself. Note that a proposition is a part of a plan or scheme, and as such must always include an activity of control, the metric.

"The trouble with 'opportunity' is that it comes disguised as hard work."

Anonymous

Quagmire

A difficult or precarious situation in management, a predicament, in which a manager or partner finds that his decision making or lack thereof have placed the company or firm at risk.

Whenever a company or firm's management finds itself in a Quagmire, it normally indicates that there is no formal line of authority between persons and departments within the company or firm, and therefore a lack of accountability for the work, tasks, and objectives of the firm or company. Understanding and utilizing the activity of accountability with metrics is the basis for not finding yourself in a Quagmire. Accountability is an activity of the Leadership function of management.

Quality

A distinguishing characteristic of products, services, or metrics which show a degree of excellence in the makeup of their functionality.

Within a management process, individuals become quality professional managers and partners by mastering the six functions of management and their activities, and applying the management tenets to their company and firm. (See Management Tenet)

"...sometimes it is better to remain quiet, and be thought a fool.... then to open your mouth and erase all doubt."

E. H. Murphy

Vocabulary & Axioms for Professional Managers and Partners
2nd Edition © Gregory N. Weismantel, 2014

R

Recommendation

That section of a proposal which has been developed from background facts and the conclusion of these facts, which is considered the best course of action for a manager or partner of a company or firm.

When the background facts and conclusion are logical steps, then the Recommendation of the proposal has a high degree of being activated. This underscores the importance of the formal decision making techniques for a Recommendation to resolve the "real problem" and not the apparent one.

Record Tracking of Accomplishment

Information or data on the accomplishment of a particular plan, objective, or metric which is collected and preserved as a history of performance or achievement of objectives and metrics.

Records of Accomplishment should be required by all managers in the implementation of key objectives, strategic action plans, and project and program objectives, since these are all critical to accomplishment of the operational and strategic objectives of the company or firm. It also allows evaluation of an individual's performance over time utilizing metrics that are proven to be realistic to the individual and to the team. (See, AXIOM of Realistic Metrics)

Relationship, Line, Direct

Direct Line Relationships are those managerial relationships which relate directly to accountability for accomplishing the mission with key objectives and metrics.

Line Relationships imply having the authority for directly making decisions to achieve the key objectives and metrics. (See Accountability, Line; Relationship, Staff)

Relationship, Line, Functional

Functional Line Relationships occur when a staff manager is directly accountable for the accomplishment of a key objective (line functionality), but maintains the direct staff accountability in the organization.

In a Functional Line Relationship there is a line accountability established for the accomplishment of that particular key objective. For example, Administration is usually a staff unit that supports the line in a company or firm, but an Administration manager or partner can be delegated accountability for a key objective of the company or firm by the CEO or Managing Partner. The Admin manager maintains his ongoing direct staff relationship to support and service the organization ongoing, but for this specific key objective he takes on a Functional Line Relationship to accomplish the key objective.

Relationship, Managerial

A specified state of affairs existing among managers and partners with their direct reports related to or dealing with one another in a company, firm, or team.

Company or firm relationships should always be considered objective relationships as opposed to subjective due to the requirement to make decisions with an open mind based upon facts. While a Managerial Relationship is important to achieve the mission of the company or firm, it should always be based upon an objective position, not a subjective one.

Relationship, Staff, Direct

Direct Staff Relationships are those managerial relationships which do not relate to accountability for accomplishing the mission, but relate to fully supporting and servicing those line managers and partners who have that accountability.

Direct Staff Relationships occur when a manager or partner must provide support and service to another unit or person in order for that unit or person to achieve the key objective. A Direct Staff Relationship exists with those units or personnel with which he or she works. This is perhaps one of the more difficult management tenets for partners and managers to comprehend, but the task is to understand that both line and staff have similar roles in accountability. (See Accountability, Staff; Relationship, Direct Line)

Relationship, Staff, Functional

Functional Staff Relationships occur when a line manager must provide support and service (staff functionality) for the accomplishment of a key objective, but maintains the direct line accountability in the organization.

As such, there is a Functional Staff Relationship established to support and serve those managers and partners who are accountable for the accomplishment of that particular key objective. For example, Sales is usually a line unit that is accountable for a key objective of the company or firm, but a Sales manager or partner takes on a Functional Staff Relationship in supporting customer service once the sale has been made, even though the Sales manager or partner maintains his ongoing direct line relationship in achieving the ongoing key objectives of the company or firm. It requires the Sales manager or partner to support customer service in every way possible.

Reporting, Action Plan

To provide a formal account or summation by a manager or partner of the results of a formal plan of action to his superior manager or partner.

Action Plan Reporting is not a step of a formal action plan, but is normal protocol of a manager or partner in reporting to a higher level of authority whenever a formal action plan is implemented.

Responsibility

Implies the trustworthy performance of fixed duties or work, and it implies that a specific person is designated to accomplish that work.

The difference between responsibility and accountability is that responsibility is only the work, whereas accountability adds authority to complete that work along with an agreement by the individual that the work will be completed to a given metric. Responsibility is a segment of activity of the Organizing function of management.

Results

The consequence of a particular action, project operation, or other course of action related to achieving an objective with metrics in a company or firm.

Results are the means by which a manager or partner implements performance evaluation and appraisal, and is an activity of the Control function of management.

Results Oriented

The type of partner or manager, line or staff, who has a penchant for achieving every objective according to an agreed-to metric, and is consistently achieving objectives within the company or firm when other managers and partners are less effective in doing so.

According to AXIOM of Management, managers get paid for achieving objectives. By definition, Results Oriented managers normally are paid more than non-results oriented managers. This would hold for partners of firms as well.

Review

To consider the quality of work completed in arrears, for the purpose of correcting performance in the future.

(See Performance Review)

"A proper command system should be able to set itself goals, and then strive to attain those goals in spite of the clear realization that things will go wrong, but also in the confidence that, when they do go wrong, the system will be able to overcome the obstacles."

General Mordehai Gur
Strategic Chief of Staff
Israel Defense Forces

S

Satisfactory Performance

In a management process, Satisfactory Performance is when a manager or partner of a company or firm meets or exceeds the metric of the objective which was agreed with a higher level of authority.

Satisfactory Performance should not be considered a level of performance but should be considered the evaluative performance required for the CEO or Managing Partner to achieve the mission of the company or firm. In the evaluation and appraisal process of managing, the appraisal process is where the degree of achievement is recognized by upper management, not the actual achievement.

Scheduling, Work

The management work of planning a list of items or forthcoming events by an accountable partner or manager in the specific order of which she wants them to occur.

Work Scheduling is an activity of the Planning function of management, and therefore management work. (See Management Work)

Segments of Management (aka Activities)

A Segment of Management is a particular type of event or activity that a manager must undertake in exercising any of the six functions of management: Strategy, Planning, Organizing, Leading, Teamwork, and Control.

Whenever one activity of a function of management is being utilized, there is at least one other activity of management being utilized at the same time. For example, whenever an individual sets the Objectives (Planning), the quality Metrics (Control) are required to be utilized to measure the accomplishment of those plans.

Selection, People

Is a segment or activity of the Organizing function of management, and the professional manager utilizes this activity as a part of the event that includes Interviewing, People Selection, Hiring and Firing.

The activity of People Selection is a functional line management accountability and should never be delegated to a staff unit to make the decision to select the person to join the company or firm.

Self-Evaluation

Is the process utilized by a direct report of a manager or partner to objectively determine if the metrics to an objective have been accomplished.

Each management level has a higher level of authority to which it is accountable, so the definition above pertains to both the manager or partner and his direct reports. (See Evaluation, Self)

Service and Support

The accountability of a staff manager or partner in relation to a line manager or partner, where the staff manager is accountable to provide complete support and service to the line manager because the line manager is directly accountable for achieving the key objectives and metrics of the company or firm.

While line and staff relationships are critical to the success of any operation, the staff accountability is always the most important to the success of the enterprise in achieving its mission, not the line accountability. This is true for the enterprise unit as well as the team unit. (See Manager, Line; Manager, Staff; Relationship Direct Line; Relationship, Direct Staff)

Skill Set

The talent of a direct report in specific areas of work or responsibility which is learned over a period of time and is an example of specialist work in which a direct report has more expertise than his or her manager.

The manager does not need to possess the Skill Sets that a particular specialist work requires, but needs to be able to utilize the six functions of management with direct reports who do have the Skill Set. We see this quite often in business, for example, when a partner in a CPA firm who is the firm's expert manager for the audit department is switched over to managing the tax department. In this instance the management skills need to be greater than the specialist skills. Any partner or manager of a company or firm who masters the functions and tenets of management can change management jobs without having vast experience knowing the specialist work. (See Specialist Work)

Social Media in Leadership Management

Are the various media that leadership managers and partners utilize to communicate online in a 2-way methodology with internal and external shareholders, stakeholders, and clients in a social, collaborative manner.

Social Media in Leadership Management includes blogs, wikis, video, photo, pdf sharing and other online devices to gain share of collaborative content versus your competition

Social Networking in Leadership Management

Occurs when leadership managers and partners create a personal profile and interact to become part of a community of similarly interested people and to share in information with internal and external shareholders, stakeholders, and clients in a social, collaborative manner.

Social networks are proliferating by the day, and the key ones for Leadership Managers at this time are LinkedIn, Facebook, and Twitter. However this will change each year into the future.

Span of Control

Is the number of direct reports that a manager or partner can adequately supervise and manage to achieve the objectives for the department she manages.

Prior to 2008 and the Great Recession, it was believed that a manager could only adequately supervise and manage a maximum of 8 people, which is the common span of control for a military squad. However since the Great Recession of 2008 managers now have a span of control which is approximately 10 or more direct reports. The professional manager in the 21st Century must now base his or her management expertise on accountability and delegating the work with authority to direct reports, and allowing direct reports to make important department decisions. Span of Control is actually an activity of the Organizing function of management, and also utilizes activities of the Control function of management.

Specialist

A direct report who has devoted himself to being the expert for a particular responsibility or work for a company or firm, and whose particular work is referred to as Specialist Work.

A Specialist utilizes the same techniques of managing his work as a manager or partner utilizes to manage his department responsibilities. That is why it is critically important that the Specialists in the company or firm receive some education on the pertinent management tenets, as well as the managers themselves.

Specialist Work

The specialist tasks performed by a person in a particular skill or specific department.

Normally the title of the individual is a sign of what specialist work the individual excels in. For example, salesman = sales; engineer = engineering work. (See Work, Management; Work, Specialist)

Staff

A group of managers, partners or direct reports who provide support and service for those line managers or partners who have the authority and are accountable for achieving the key objectives of the company or firm.

In a company or firm, the better the staff, the more successful the company or firm. Unfortunately it always appears that the line units have more fun in business than the staff units, because line has the authority to make decisions to achieve the key objectives related to the mission of the company or firm. C'est la vie, but the empirical evidence of analyzing successful companies always leads to the fact that <u>the staff is more important than the line</u>. The CEO or Managing Partner should therefore focus on having the best staff units that money can buy, and require demanding metrics on the staff units for support and servicing the line.

Stratagem

In business, a formal tactical maneuver designed to deceive or surprise a competitor and which is a critical part of a strategic plan of an enterprise.

Stratagem are confidential tactics which are used by managers and partners of a company or firm to disguise a perceived strength or weakness of the organization within a competitive marketplace. It is as important for the manager or partner to use stratagems to disguise the strength of the company or firm as it is to use stratagems to disguise the weaknesses.

Strategic Action Plans

For strategic planning, Strategic Action Plans are those annual plans with metrics that address resolving critical issues and accomplish a segment of the strategic plan for one of the three (3) years of the plan.

Strategic Action Plans are placed into the current operational plan to resolve key strategic issues that have been identified in strategy. They are so important to the company or firm that only key partners and executive managers should be accountable for accomplishing Strategic Action Plans, and the individuals so accountable should have their bonus and profit sharing tied to their accomplishment.

Strategic Assumptions

In strategic planning, Strategic Assumptions are statements accepted or supposed true without complete proof or evidence and which must be substantiated or revised during each operational year of the strategic plan of the company or firm.

Strategic Assumptions must be researched and flushed out as close to true as is possible, and usually are based upon competitive products, services, and competitive marketing in relation to the company or firm's current products and services. The reason that the first year of the strategic plan is actually this year's operational plan is because Strategic Assumptions are confirmed during the operational year, and revised for succeeding years of the strategic plan. (See Axiom of Competitive Products and Services)

Strategic Initiative (See Strategic Plan)

Strategic Management (See Management, Strategic)

Strategic Plan

Is a continuous plan designed and implemented by the CEO and the Vice Presidents of a company, or the Managing Partner and other key Partners of a firm, which is a general maneuver or approach by the company or firm to accomplish visionary objectives over a 3-year period.

While implementing strategy involves the Strategy Function of management, Strategic Plans involve the Planning Function of management. There are two important points involving a Strategic Plan: 1) it is the executive management team who is completely accountable for the strategic action plans which will accomplish the strategy, all having line accountability; 2) Year 1 of the Strategic Plan is actually the operational plan of that year.

Strategically

The most important or essential stratagem in relation to strategy, and essential to effective tactics in reducing or neutralizing competitive products and services of a company or firm.

Professional managers and partners utilize planned stratagem versus their competition by forecasting and predicting what will impact the organization's driving force and utilizing strategic assumptions. The result is a dynamic combination of strategy mixed with formal operational plans that explode into successful momentum for a company or firm. (See Stratagem; Strategic Assumptions)

Strategy

Is the art that a manager or partner must have in using stratagem in strategic management so that the operational objectives with metrics will be achieved.

While it is not essential that a CEO or Managing Partner utilize strategy and strategic planning to be successful in operational management, the clear evidence is that those companies and firms that combine strategic planning with operational planning are the more successful companies and firms. (See Plans, Operational; Plans, Strategic)

Supervise

To direct and inspect the performance of specialist work as it relates to the responsibilities of individuals in a company or firm. (See Control by Inspection)

Supervisor

Any first line manager who has the accountability of supervising a number of direct reports that perform specialist work in a company or firm.

Supervisors are normally doer-managers and are normally the first line of management within a company or firm. The best executive managers and partners are normally those who have progressed from being solid supervisors, doers, into managers that achieve objectives through and with others in the organization or firm. (See Manager, Doer)

Sycophant Manager (or Partner)

A manager of a company or a partner of a firm who attempts to win favor or advance his or her position by flattering other managers or partners of higher authority, particularly those with higher influence on the Sycophant Manager's ranking within the firm or company.

In a properly structured management process within a company or firm, with cascading objectives and metrics throughout the organization, a Sycophant Manager or Partner will have a difficult time achieving their objectives as long as the metrics are considered "stretch" and not easy to achieve. (See Yes Man; Cascading Objectives)

Synergistic Operations

In operational management, the actions that two or more companies, firms, or departments utilize to achieve an effect of which each is individually incapable by themselves.

While Synergistic Operations normally relate to operational management, they also are considered in strategic management when the future driving force of the company or firm will be different than the current driving force, primarily observed for merger and acquisition strategies.

System, Management

A group of interacting, interrelated, or interdependent functions of management forming a complex whole.

A Management System is the same as a management process, utilizing the six functions of management that include tenets of management. (See Management Process)

"…I cannot tell you the secret to success, but I can tell you the secret to failure: try to please everyone."

Anonymous

Tactful

Showing the ability to appreciate the sensitivity of a business or personal situation by saying the most appropriate and fitting words and gestures, which may also suggest the use of stratagem.

Being Tactful by a manager or partner is essential in being promoted to succeeding levels of management within a company or firm. (See Stratagem)

Tactical

A management technique characterized by finesse and expertise in maneuvering to achieve the mission of the firm or company.

The ability for a manager or partner to be Tactical in achieving objectives is determined by the ability to recognize the real problem versus the apparent problem in decision making, and then provide the finesse required to lead a company or firm in implementing an action plan with metrics that achieves the objectives and metrics of the company and firm.

Tactics

The work or technique that a manager or partner utilizes for achieving the objective, often designated by strategy.

A Tactic is a segment or activity of operational management, and is used by a manager or partner to utilize management tenets with the specialist work of the department to achieve objectives with metrics.

Task

A piece of specialist work assigned by a manager or partner to a direct report, or performed as part of a direct report's ongoing responsibilities.

The professional manager and partner in the 21st Century should always assign the responsibility (objective) with an agreed-to measurement (metric) which will determine the accomplishment of the responsibility by both the direct report and the manager or partner.

Task Force

The grouping of a company or firm's human and physical resources for the accomplishment of a specific objective with metrics, normally on a temporary and time denoted basis.

While the term Task Force is utilized more in the military, its use in the 21st Century organization occurs with the use of cross-functional teams when specific human and physical resources from disparate departments are garnered together to achieve a specific objective, which is usually more strategic than operational. (See Team, Cross-Functional)

Task Master

A manager or partner who imposes difficult specialist work and metrics on an organization to achieve the objectives of the company or firm.

A Task Master has a negative connotation in many companies and firms, so a manager or partner should be aware of being referred to as a Task Manager.

Team

A number of individuals with similar or different characteristics and skill sets that have a common leader who has the authority to accomplish a mission with objectives and metrics.

The best teams are formed in a firm or company by first staffing them with the experts who know and understand the specialist work that must be accomplished to achieve the team's objective. These are normally the workers who report to the partners and managers. A Team is not a group. (See Group)

Team Accountability

A description of the purpose of the team as it relates to the responsibility and authority which a team undertakes in accomplishing its mission or purpose.

Team Accountability also cascades down through the team, exactly like the process of management has objectives and metrics from the highest to the lowest level of the organization. (See, Cascading of Objectives)

Team Empowerment

Is the term used to describe the training of individuals on the team to accomplish objectives with metrics as a team, with emphasis on team accountability.

By far the best method of training individuals to become active participants on a team is to have each of them understand the full meaning of accountability, and how it functions with a team leader. Team Empowerment is when the team leader delegates the work or responsibility of the team to its members, along with the authority to complete the work. Another level of accountability is established.

Team Leader

A designated member of a team who has been delegated the work and objectives of a project as well as the authority to complete the work from a higher level of authority, and who has agreed to accept that responsibility and authority to achieve the objectives according to agreed-upon metrics.

A Team Leader could be chosen by the team prior to being delegated the work and the authority to complete the work; or could be designated by an executive or partner with authority to create the team. In either instance, team delegation has occurred to accomplish the objective of the team. "Team Leader" is a misnomer because it implies that the individual will only lead the team which has been organized to accomplish the objective, and not manage the team. In effect a Team Leader must be the highest qualified individual in understanding management work, particularly accountability and managing with metrics, than the normal level of managers within the company or firm.

Team, Cross Functional

A group of direct reports, each the expert in different specialist work responsibilities, working together toward a common objective of the company or firm.

Cross Functional Teams utilize the activities of the Organizing function of management, along with the Teamwork function of management. The manager or partner of the 21st Century is required to achieve more objectives with fewer resources, and utilizing Cross Functional Teams is a method utilized by successful firms and companies in achieving complex objectives with metrics.

Teamwork

To take harmonious action in a unified or "team" effort for obtaining active help, cooperation, understanding, and *agreement from another person, department or segment of the business, <u>over which there is no authority.</u>*

Teamwork is one of the six functions of management, and infers a cooperative and collaborative effort by the members of a group or team to achieve a common objective with metrics in line and staff relationships. Because of the diversity of skill sets usually found on a team, Teamwork is always a combination of line and staff accountability, with individuals playing specific roles. At one point a team member might have line accountability to accomplish a step of the team plan, while other members would have staff accountability to support the individual in doing so. Understanding the line and staff relationships of management linked with accountability is key to successful teamwork. (See Relationship, Direct Line; Relationship, Direct Staff)

Teamwork, Function of Management (See Function of Management, Teamwork)

Teamwork, Participatory

The act of taking part or accepting accountability for various responsibilities within a team's objectives and metrics.

The team leader (manager) is accountable to insure that each team member is afforded the opportunity for individual participation in achieving the team's objectives and metrics. If this delegation of responsibility and authority does not occur then the team leader remains accountable for the work required to achieve that segment of the objective and metric.

Technique of Sound Decision Making

Seven steps that a professional manager or partner in the 21st Century utilizes for making solid decisions during the problem solving process.

The Technique of Sound Decision Making includes 1) Stating the apparent problem; 2) Problem Sensitivity in determining what normally is the situation versus the apparent problem; 3) Finding the Critical Factor of the problem by asking who, what, where, why, etc.; 4) Defining the real problem; 5) Establishing Vital Sign of the problem for determining proper metrics; 6) Determining the alternatives to resolve the problem; and 7) Developing the Key Decision Point, what we can do, not necessarily what we want to do.

Technique, Management
The techniques that a manager or partner utilizes with their direct reports to achieve objectives and have superior results from their direct reports in doing so.

Management Techniques can be trained, but utilization still requires a manager or partner to understand how the techniques fit into activities of the functions of management. For example, techniques of decision making are shown in training sessions, but utilizing the technique in problem solving is usually developed by the professional manager or partner in real life examples.

Tenet, Management (See Management Tenet)

Time Denoted Plans (See Plans, Time Denoted)

Tolerable Limits
Parameters of authority which are established by a manager or partner with his or her subordinate(s) within which the subordinate(s) can work without consulting the manager or partner.

By utilizing Tolerable Limits a manager or partner reduces the risk of a subordinate's inexperience in certain specialist work and increases the capability of the subordinate to accomplish the objective. A manager or partner utilizing Tolerable Limits has become staff to his own subordinate, and must provide training to insure that the objective is completed according to the metrics prescribed. (See, Relationship, Functional Staff)

Tracing the Line of Authority

The failsafe process that a manager or partner utilizes to determine the accountable person or department for a particular responsibility or work in the company or firm.

Since accountability includes the work and the authority provided by a higher level of authority in the company or firm, the failsafe process includes a mere tracing of the authority for that work from the higher level to the lower level, which determines the accountable individual or department of the company or firm.

Training

To make proficient skill sets of an individual of the company or firm with specialized instruction and practice on a skill set of specialist work, not management work.

Training is an activity of the Leading function of management. Each manager or partner is line accountable for training the direct reports of his department, team, or unit, regardless whether his unit is a line or staff organization. Training is 90% company driven, and 10% individual driven; while development is 90% individual driven and 10% company driven. (See Management Development)

"Management by objective works – if you know the objectives."
Peter Drucker

"Sorry Peter, that's not what happened!
Everyone knew the objectives. MBO was missing the one critical ingredient of Control – the agreed-to metric between manager and subordinate - that measured the accomplishment! MBO then forced the creation of a Leadership Management activity entitled 'conflict resolution.' "

Greg Weismantel

Vocabulary & Axioms for Professional Managers and Partners
2nd Edition © Gregory N. Weismantel, 2014

U

Uncritical-Many Factors

The 5-10 factors which are the most <u>unimportant</u> ingredients to accomplishing the objective of the team.

The "critical few factors" as opposed to the "uncritical many factors" is the adage for managers and partners in the 21st century, when resources are at a minimum. (See Critical Few Factors)

Understanding Communications

In the activity of communication, Understanding Communications is the activity of the receiver of the message to comprehend the meaning of the message from the sender, so that the receiver can respond back with a meaningful response to the sender, thereby making perfect communication.

Communications is an activity of the Leading function of management, and a manager or partner must always strive to be the best communicator in order to achieve the most objectives with their direct reports.

Undisputed Measurement

Is a metric which has no other possibility of measuring the accomplishment of an objective and is therefore an Undisputed Measurement of the accomplishment of the objective.

For example, the perfect measurement to determine whether any apple is ripe is to crack it open and see if the seeds are brown, no matter what type or variety of apple. That would be considered the Undisputed Measurement of an objective. (See KPI, Key Performance Indicator)

Variable Metric
A metric which fluctuates directly with output changes.
While it is not recommended that Variable Metrics be utilized by a manager or partner with direct reports, there are certain circumstances which require the use of Variable Metrics, particularly when the objective is subject to fluctuation.

Variance of the Metric
In a management process, the difference between what is expected to occur in a measurement and what actually occurs.
Use of Key Performance Indicators (KPI) allow variances to be recorded and adjusted for measuring future objectives in the same area.

Vision
The talent of a general manager, usually a CEO or a Managing Partner of a company or firm, who has unusual competence in discerning the future direction of the company or firm based upon prescient knowledge and intelligent foresight.
Vision is a segment of activity of the Strategy function of management. (See Prescient Manager)

Vital Signs of the Objective

The most significant traits of the objective that can be identified by the manager or partner. These traits are called the Vital Signs of the Objective, and are the basis for developing strong measurements (metrics) for the accomplishment of the objective.

Just as the human body has vital signs such as temperature, pulse rate, blood pressure, etc., with corresponding metrics (98.6 degrees F; 60 beats per minute; 120/80 pressure) the objective also has such vital signs which drive the development of strong metrics for the manager or partner as well as their direct reports.

Wasted Effort

A useless or worthless by-product of expending the motivational energy of a team or unit in resolving a problem or issue which is impacting the achievement of key objectives of the CEO or Managing Partner of the company or firm.

Wasted Effort is what occurs when a manager or partner does not utilize a formal technique of decision making such that the team or unit begins work on the apparent problem or symptom, and not the real problem that requires correction. (See, Problem, Apparent)

Work

The responsibility of physical or mental effort or activity directed toward the production or accomplishment of an objective. This can be in the form of Specialist Work or Management Work. (See Work, Management; Work, Specialist)

Work, Management

The work that managers perform in the six functions of management, and their corresponding activities: Strategy, Planning, Organizing, Leading, Teamwork, and Control.

The most difficult work is Management Work, because of a manager or partner's accountability for the key objectives of the mission. (Also see Key Objectives; Specialist Work; Management Work)

Work, Specialist

The specialist tasks performed by a person in a particular skill or specific department.

Normally the title of the individual is a sign of what specialist work the individual excels in. For example, salesman = sales; engineer = engineering work. (See Work, Management;)

Worm's-Eye View

A close-up view by an individual who is an expert at the specialist work in which there is a problem that requires specific actions by someone who can identify the real problem from the apparent problem.

In decision making and problem solving, the Worm's-Eye View by the specialist expert normally is critical in identifying the real problem from the apparent problem.

X-Axis

The horizontal axis of a Cartesian coordinate system, or one of three axes in a three-dimensional Cartesian coordinate system.

(See XY Relationship; Y-Axis; Z-Axis)

X-Factor

The unknown function, thing, or event which provides a manager or partner with an advantageous ability often regarded as mysterious and unique to duplicate by your competition.

In a management process the X-Factor is always seen as a manager or partner understanding and implementing the activity of accountability with metrics within their organization, which is always attributed to mysterious and difficult insight by an individual, but is in actuality the quality of a manager or partner developing and utilizing the six functions of management. The X-Factor is often seen during the development of a company or firm's strategic plan. (See Prescient Manager; Stratagem)

XY Relationship

An output on a graph that a manager or partner utilizes to sketch the relationship between two variables on a grid of plane rectangular coordinates in order to analyze the impact of each variable upon another.

An XY Relationship allows a manager or partner to track one variable to determine the impact on another variable during the same time period such that behavior patterns of work and accountability can be shown. One such relationship has been identified in the variable of communications with the variable teamwork, and an axiom has been developed to identify that the amount of communication required by a team is in proportion to the amount of teamwork and coordination required by the team objective. (See Axiom of Communication Requirements)

Yammer

To complain and whine constantly so that the manager, partner or the team is distracted from placing the proper steps to resolve the real problem in the technique of logical decision making.

In teamwork, some team individuals are known to yammer because they do not have the authority to make decisions, and whine consistently about the process. It is better for the team leader (manager) to eliminate the yammering individual from the team rather than keep the individual actively working on the team.

Yard

A tract of hardscape parking areas surrounding a warehouse, often enclosed, in which a warehouse manager receives and ships merchandise into its distribution channel from truck and rail transportation units.

Often in a warehouse management system (WMS) the warehouse manager will manage a process designed to maximize receiving shipments into the warehouse with shipments of products out of the warehouse.

Y-Axis

The vertical axis of a Cartesian coordinate system, or one of three axes in a three-dimensional Cartesian coordinate system.

(See XY Relationship; X-Axis)

Year End, Fiscal

The end of the fiscal year for a business or firm in which final profitability is determined.

In a management process, the Fiscal Year End is the time period that time-denoted annual objectives are evaluated as achieved or not achieved by the management team. (See Evaluate; and Evaluate, Self)

Yes Man

A manager or partner reporting to another manager or partner of the company or firm with greater authority, who constantly agrees with one's superior without questioning.

(See Sycophant Manager or Partner)

Yo-Yo Manager or Partner

A manager or partner who constantly vacillates on decision making and moves repeatedly from one position to another during the process.

A Yo-Yo Manager or Partner is always recognized by his subordinates as being indecisive and unsure of himself in making decisions. Such a manager or partner often compensates for this management weakness by appointing committees to facilitate the decision making and problem solving process within the company or firm. The solution to this weakness in a manager or partner is to master the Technique of Sound Decision Making on a formal basis. (See Technique of Sound Decision Making)

Z-Axis

One of three axes in a three-dimensional Cartesian coordinate system.

(See XY Relationship; X-Axis; Y-Axis)

Zero Based Budgeting

Zero Based Budgeting is the financial management <u>planning</u> process by which each manager or partner identifies and justifies each line item expense of his accountability's budget as well as the financial resources required to support that line item expense of the budget.

Zero Based Budgeting is normally utilized within smaller sub-functional groups of an organization which have high accountability for achieving the team objectives as well as the financial parameters for those objectives. Note that Zero Based Budgeting is an activity of the Planning function of management.

Zero-Defect

Within a company, Zero-Defect is utilized as the <u>metric</u> by which quality assurance (QA) or quality control (QC) departments allow the acceptance of vendor products to be placed into the company's inventory, or which a manufacturer of products can produce a product to ship to its customers or clients with minimal inspection.

Zero-Defect products are normally those requiring high precision in utilization by professional organizations such as doctors and engineers. Note that Zero-Defect is a "metric" which is an activity of the Control function of management.

Zilch
Zero, nothing, nada; an insignificant person; nonentity; amounting to nothing.

In an effort to add more "Z's" to the vocabulary of managers and partners, Zilch was determined to fit several managerial definitions: 1) When a manager or partner receives Zilch for a bonus or annual share of profits, it reflects directly on his or her ability to achieve strategic and operational objectives according to agreed-to metrics; and 2) when a manager or partner is called "Zilch" by other managers or partners it is a derogatory term implying zero, nothing, an empty suit or dress, not a description of George Costanza of Seinfeld.

Terms in the Vocabulary

Accept

Accepting

Accountability, Definition of

Accountability, Line

Accountability, Requirements for

Accountability, Staff

Accrued Authority

Acculturation of Management

Administer Responsibilities

Advise

Agreement in Accountability

Analogous Practicality

Analyze

Apparent Problem (See Problem, Apparent)

Appraisal

Approval

Art of Management

Aspect of the Problem

Assessment of Alternatives

Assignment

Assistant Manager (Partner)

Associate Manager (Partner)
Assumed Authority
Assumptions of Strategy
Audit, Financial
Audit of Management Tenets
Authority
Authority, Line of (See Line of Authority)
Authority, Objective
Authority, Subjective
Authorize
Axiom

Board of Directors
Board of Directors, Accountabilities
Board of Directors, Advisory (See Advisory Board)
Board of Directors, Delegation
Board of Directors, Responsibilities
Bonus, Employee
Bonus, Performance
Brainstorm
Break-Even Point
Budget
Budgeting Scheme
Bureaucracy
Bureaucrat

Business Units

Cascading of Objectives
Coach
Collaboration of Duties
Collaborative Failure
Command Authority
Commitment
Committee
Communicating Efficiently
Communication in Teamwork
Communication, One Way
Communication, Two Way
Company
Conclusion
Conduct, Management
Consolidation, Organization
Consultant
Consultant, Management
Control
Control by the 20/80 Rule
Control by the 80/20 Rule
Coordination, External
Coordination, Internal

Core Process
Critical Factors
Critical Few Factors
Culture of the Company or Firm

Decide
Decision
Decision Making, Centralized
Decision Making, Decentralized
Decision Making, Logical
Decision Making, Natural
Decisive
Definition
Delegate
Delegation
Delegator Manager (See Manager, Delegator)
Delineation of Management Levels
Developing Direct Reports
Development, Manager
Direct Reports
Directive Statement
Divisions, Corporate
Drill Down of Objectives
Driving Force(s)

Driving Force, Current
Driving Force, Future

Elementary Tenets
Empowerment
Enterprise, Business
Enterprising
Environment, Business External
Environment, Business Internal
Evaluation
Evaluation, Manager (Partner)
Evaluation, Self-
Exception, Control by
Exception, Metric
Execution
Executive Agreement
Executive Council
Executive Decree
Executive Manager (Partner)
Executive Primer Program
Expectation

F

Feedback, Brainstorm
Follow Through
Forecasting
Function of Management, Control
Function of Management, Control Segments
Function of Management, Leading
Function of Management, Leading Segments
Function of Management, Organizing
Function of Management, Organizing Segments
Function of Management, Planning
Function of Management, Planning Segments
Function of Management, Strategy
Function of Management, Strategy Segments
Function of Management, Teamwork
Function of Management, Teamwork Segments
Function, Work
Functions of Management

G

Game Changer Events
Goal
Group
Guide, Management

H

Habilitation, Management
Habitual Techniques
Habituated Management Tenets
Half-Cocked Manager (Or Partner)
Hardball Manager (Or Partner)
Havoc, Organizational
Hierarchy, Business Organization

I

Identifying Vital Signs
Input for Planning
Interpretation, Work
Issue or Problem
Issue or Problem, Apparent
Issue or Problem, Real

Job Description
Job Enhancement
Job Knowledge
Job or Task

Key Decision Point
Key Objectives and Metrics
Key Performance Indicators – KPI
Kibitzer

L

Leader, Business
Leader, Management
Leader, Team (See Team Leader)
Leadership
Leadership Attributes
Leadership Management
Leadership Management, Stages of
Leadership Style
Leading
Level, Manager
Line Correlation
Line of Authority
Logic Gap

M

Management Attitude or Disposition
Management Authority
Management by Objectives (MBO)
Management Depth
Management Development

Management Process
Management Tenet
Management Training
Management Work
Management, Assumptive
Management, Operations
Management, Science of
Management, Strategic
Manager
Manager Vs. Leader
Manager, Delegator
Manager, Doer
Manager, Executive (Partner)
Manager, First Line
Manager, General
Manager, Line (Or Partner)
Manager, Middle
Manager, Professional
Manager, Staff (Or Partner)
Measurable Objectives
Measure
Mentor, Management
Mentor, Specialist
Metric
Metric, Qualitative
Metric, Quantitative
Metrics, Development of
Mission
Mission Statement
Motivation

Motivation, Compelling

Motivation, Encouragement

Motivation, Impelling

Motivation, Incentive or Money

Motivation, Inspire

Motivation, Using Bonus for

Motivation, Using Money For

Multi-Faceted Metric

Nameplate, Manager's (Or Partner's)

Narrative, Manager

Natural Decision Making

Negotiation

Network, Manager (Or Partner)

Objective Evaluation

Objective, Annual (aka Fiscal)

Objective, Key

Objective, Operational

Objective, Strategic

Objectives, Establishment of Annual

Objectives, Establishment of Ongoing (Continuous)

Occurrence, Abnormal

Occurrence, Normal

Operational

Operationalization

Operator

Order

Organization Chart

Organization, Business

Organization, Integrated

Organization, Matrix

Organization, Most Effective

Organization, Most Efficient

Organizational Structure

Organizational, Restructuring

Organizing

Organizing Around the People

Organizing Around the Work

Outcome

Output

Paradigm, Management

Performance

Performance Appraisal

Performance Correcting

Performance Evaluation

Performance Evaluation, Satisfactory

Performance Evaluation, Unsatisfactory

Performance Metrics

Performance Metrics, Development of

Performance Review

Persona, Company or Firm

Plan

Planning

Plans, Action

Plans, Action, Strategic

Plans, Fiscal Year

Plans, Individual Ongoing

Plans, Long Range

Plans, Ongoing or Continuous

Plans, Operational

Plans, Project

Plans, Strategic

Plans, Time-Denoted

Pockets of Work

Policy, Company or Firm

Position

Position Description (See Job Description)

Position, Manager

Position, Specialist

Power

Power Structure

Powerless

Prescient Manager (Or Partner)
Present Alternatives
Price Elasticity
Problem
Problem Analysis
Problem Solving
Problem, Apparent
Problem, Real
Procedure, Business
Procedures, Problems with
Process, Management
Process, Operational
Professional Manager
Profit
Profit Center
Profit Formula
Profit Sharing
Program
Program Plans
Proliferation, Negative
Proliferation, Positive
Proposal
Proposition

Q

Quagmire
Quality

R

Recommendation
Record Tracking of Accomplishment
Relationship, Line, Direct
Relationship, Line, Functional
Relationship, Managerial
Relationship, Staff, Direct
Relationship, Staff, Functional
Reporting, Action Plan
Responsibility
Results
Results Oriented
Review

S

Satisfactory Performance

Scheduling, Work

Segments of Management

Selection, People

Self-Evaluation

Service and Support

Skill Set

Social Media in Leadership Management
Social Networking in Leadership Management
Span of Control

Specialist

Specialist Work

Staff

Stratagem

Strategic Action Plan

Strategic Assumptions

Strategic Initiative (See Strategic Plan)

Strategic Management

Strategic Plan

Strategically

Strategy

Supervise

Supervisor

Sycophant Manager (or Partner)

Synergistic Operations

System, Management

T

Tactful

Tactical

Tactics

Task

Task Force

Task Master

Team

Team Accountability

Team Empowerment

Team Leader

Team, Cross Functional

Teamwork

Teamwork, Function of management

Teamwork, Participatory

Technique of Sound Decision Making

Technique, Management

Tenet, Management

Time Denoted Plans (See Plans, Time Denoted)

Tolerable Limits

Tracing the Line of Authority

Training

Uncritical-Many Factors
Understanding Communications
Undisputed Measurement

Variable Metric
Variance of the Metric
Vision
Vital Signs of the Objective

Wasted Effort
Work
Work, Management
Work, Specialist

Worm's-Eye View

X-Axis
X-Factor
XY Relationship

Yammer
Yard
Y-Axis
Year End, Fiscal
Yes Man
Yo-Yo Manager or Partner

Z-Axis
Zero Based Budgeting
Zero-Defect
Zilch

"...Lead, follow....
or get out of the way."

General George Patton

AXIOMS IN MANAGEMENT TENETS

An axiom in leadership management is a self-evident and accepted principle concerning a defined activity of management. (See Management Tenet)

Axioms in leadership management are critical principles that have been proven by actual managers and partners over a period of years, and not a part of unproven theory developed by academia. For over 30 years the Epic Management Group of consultants has analyzed every tenet of management by working with managers and partners of all sizes of companies and firms throughout the United States and Canada. Through this hands-on process we have recognized that there are certain Tenets of Management which all successful companies implement, and the result of our findings occur in what we term AXIOMs in Management Tenets.

Our experience has shown that successful companies all address Strategic and Operational Management in the same regimented approach, much like a successful football team always utilizes correct blocking and tackling skills when being continuously successful. If you cannot block and tackle properly, you cannot win! The same is true in management. If a manager or partner does not understand and practice the "blocking and tackling of AXIOMs in Management Tenets" the odds are that the manager or partner will not be as successful as his or her colleagues who do.

The following areas are where we have developed Axioms in Management Tenets based upon our observations over 30 years with real companies and their CEOs and Managing Partners:

1. The Progression of Managers from Doers to Achievers Through Others
2. The Process of Leadership Management
3. The Function of Leadership Management: Strategy
4. The Function of Leadership Management: Planning
5. The Function of Leadership Management: Organizing
6. The Function of Leadership Management: Leading
7. The Function of Leadership Management: Teamwork
8. The Function of Leadership Management: Control

Successful leadership managers and partners in the 21st Century will study and practice AXIOMs in Management Tenets while utilizing a proven vocabulary which every professional manager and partner should comprehend.

Greg Weismantel

Strategy

Planning

Organizing

Leadership

Teamwork

Control

The DNA of a Manager & Partner

Vocabulary & Axioms for Professional Managers and Partners
2nd Edition © Gregory N. Weismantel, 2014

"If you do not change the direction you are headed, you will end up where you are going."

Anonymous

THE PROGRESSION OF MANAGERS & PARTNERS

AXIOMS IN MANAGEMENT TENETS:
MANAGEMENT PROGRESSION

Normally, managers and partners receive a higher paycheck than non-managers and non-partners, and the main reason is the amount of accountability that a manager or partner has over a non-manager and non-partner. Managers often participate in a "Management Incentive Plan" based upon the profits of the company, not the sales; Partners usually participate in profit sharing.

The following Axioms in Management Tenets are used by successful CEOs and Managing Partners in developing their managers and partners in a company and firm.

AXIOM OF
THE BEST LEADERSHIP MANAGERS

Those individuals who overwhelmingly excel at the Specialist Work of their position seldom become the managers who overwhelmingly excel at the Management Work of the company or firm.

- The best salesman does not necessarily make the best sales manager. Same is true with any specialist field of work.

AXIOM OF
MANAGEMENT ACCOMPLISHMENT

Managers and partners are paid to accomplish the key objectives of the company or firm. The more key objectives of the company or firm that are achieved by a manager or partner, the more value that individual brings to the organization.

- If a manager or partner does not consistently achieve key objectives, the need value diminishes significantly over time.

AXIOM OF
MANAGEMENT COMPENSATION

All managers and partners are compensated to achieve more objectives than non-managers and non-partners, and higher levels of management are compensated to achieve more objectives than lower levels of management.

- The higher a manager or partner progresses within a company or firm, the more objectives are "expected" to be achieved. Since managers and partners are paid to achieve objectives, what actions should they take to max-out in pay, bonus, or profits? Well, they usually do.
- CEOs and Managing Partners should have a vested interest in combining Strategic Management with Operational Management, because maximum objectives are accomplished for a company or firm in a marketplace.

AXIOM OF
MANAGEMENT GROWTH

A "doer" achieves objectives by using innate ability as well as the specialist knowledge of the work involved. Management growth occurs when a manager or partner achieves the objective through and with others on the team, with less emphasis on using the doer's innate ability and skills, and more emphasis on using the ability and skills of the team.

- A Doer-Manager or Partner usually has some tell-tale signs for the CEO or Managing Partner to see:
    o High stack of paper on desk: poor delegator
    o Subordinates not working: waiting for you
    o Late meeting objectives: not using the team

AXIOM OF
MANAGEMENT ACHIEVEMENT

Managers and partners achieve a greater number of objectives when working through and with others, rather than using their own innate ability and specialist knowledge.

- What incentive does a manager or partner have in working through and with others? More people to achieve the manager or partner's objectives.
- Analysis shows that normally a professional manager or partner can achieve more objectives working through and with others by a factor of 8x.

AXIOM OF
INNATE ABILITY

Managers tend to gravitate back to the "doer" level, using their own innate ability and specialist knowledge rather than maximizing their results through and with others.

- The manager or partner has a comfort level of doing the specialist work for which they were hired
- Tell- tale signs of this occurring:
    - o Not meeting action plan dates agreed to
    - o Continual delays in meeting plan dates
    - o Needing to spend overtime in the office

AXIOM OF
MANAGEMENT HIERARCHY

The higher a manager or partner progresses in a company or firm, the less specialist knowledge and innate ability is required to achieve objectives.

- What actions should a manager or partner take to be the best?
    - o Focus on the critical few objectives, not the uncritical many
    - o Insure that your team or department is achieving the most objectives that are possible to achieve
    - o Delegate all specialist work down to lower levels

AXIOM OF
THE NEW RULES OF COLLABORATION

Those CEOs and Managing Partners who utilize new rules of collaboration which coincide with the use of social media and social networking principles of David Meerman Scott will be viewed more favorable by their shareholders, stakeholders, and clients in a social, collaborative manner.

- These new rules of collaboration include instant 2-way communication, and when managers and partners master these techniques they become essential business builders for their companies and firms.

AXIOM OF
COLLABORATIVE FAILURE

Those CEOs and Managing Partners who empower their innovation teams to fail in a constructive manner will normally achieve more emerging products and services than those who make failure a fear to success.

- It is often pointed out that the famous entrepreneur J. C. Penny failed seven times with his team before achieving success in the retail clothing industry.
- Penny often proclaimed that the first six failures worked all the failure bugs out of the team's plans, so that success was inevitable

"In this rapidly changing world you need to listen; otherwise you won't be able to survive."

David Meerman Scott
The New Rules of Marketing & PR

THE PROCESS OF
LEADERSHIP MANAGEMENT

AXIOMS IN MANAGEMENT TENETS:
THE LEADERSHIP
MANAGEMENT PROCESS

Through the years we have recognized that the successful companies and firms have a lot more formality than those less successful, and inevitably the employees themselves prefer working at these companies because the process is transparent and easy. It is when the process is not transparent and appears to be rigged behind closed doors that a company or firm loses its employees, either physically or mentally.

The following Axioms in Management Tenets are used by successful CEOs and Managing Partners in the process of Leadership Management.

AXIOM OF
FORMAL OBJECTIVES AND METRICS:

Those companies and firms who manage their business operationally with formal objectives and metrics are always more successful in accomplishing the mission than those companies who do not use formal objectives and metrics.

- It is the metric that is the most critical for successful CEOs and Managing Partners, and when the metric is formally written out for all to see, there is a team dynamic which insulates the organization from failure

AXIOM OF SUCCESS

Those companies and firms that combine a strategic direction with operational management are consistently more successful than those who do not.

- The reason for this is because Leadership Management achieves objectives through and with others, and this axiom projects that the vision and purpose of the company or firm combine into operational teamwork that is unbeatable

AXIOM OF
EMPLOYEE REWARD & RECOGNITION

The rate in which an employee receives rewards and recognition is in direct proportion to the amount of value in which the individual brings to the organization.

- In most instances, the value of the individual to the organization is dependent upon the number of objectives achieved ongoing by the individual

FUNCTION OF LEADERSHIP-MANAGEMENT: STRATEGY

AXIOMS IN MANAGEMENT TENETS:
STRATEGY

Strategy

Is the art that a manager or partner must have in using stratagem in strategic management so that the operational objectives with metrics will be achieved.

While it is not essential that a CEO or Managing Partner utilize strategy and strategic planning to be successful in operational management, the clear evidence is that those companies and firms that combine strategic planning with operational planning are the more successful companies and firms.

The following Axioms in Management Tenets are used by successful CEOs and Managing Partners in implementing their long term strategy.

AXIOM OF
BUSINESS STRATEGY:

If the planned strategy of a company or firm is correct, any number of tactical leadership mistakes will not impact the overall success of its mission.

- Combining Operational Management with Strategic Management creates the most successful companies and firms

AXIOM OF
SUCCESSFUL VISION

The degree in which a strategic vision within a strategy of a CEO or Managing Partner is successful is in direct proportion to the amount of input which the organization's executives have in developing it.

- Empowering the organization to critique and have input to the vision of the CEO or Managing Partner will provide the inherent commitment of the people who must execute the operational plans and metrics to achieve it.

- It does not take intelligence to create the greatest vision, in fact those visionaries are usually smarter than they are intelligent, and have a driven sense to see through obstacles which impede progress.

AXIOM OF
COMPANY, MARKETS, & PRODUCTS:

The company, its markets, and its products and services all exist within parallel life-cycle quadrants of Emerging, Growth, Maturing and Aging quadrants with correlating metrics for each.

- This does not mean that a company residing in one quadrant cannot have products & services in other quadrants

Four Phases of a Company or Firm, Market, Product or Service

EMERGING	AGING
Less than 3 yrs. old Growth in excess of 30%-50% LY No competitor with dominant Share of Market (SOM)	More than 5 years old Little or no growth 3 or 4 major competitors, none dominant, all departing until one remains before market dies
More than 3 years old Growth in excess of 20% Last Year 2-3 competitors with equal SOM	No particular age limit Less than 10% Growth Last Year At least 1 Dominant Market Leader, and at least 1 Major Competitor
GROWTH	MATURING

- The life-cycle of a company or firm mirrors the quadrant in which its markets, products and services are found.
- It is a logical progression for a company to move through its life-cycle and eventually end up in the Aging quadrant, where it ceases to exist.

AXIOM OF
BUSINESS LIFE-CYCLES

The logical progression of any company or firm is from startup or emerging, to growth, to maturing, and to aging and decline, and there can be no escaping the final aging and decline of a company or firm over time, only sustaining itself as long as its products and services reflect current customer persona.

- Eastman Kodak, Circuit City, Enron, and others all went through the four quadrants of their life cycle. It is the accountability of the CEO to sustain a company's growth products and services so that it can remain viable for as long as possible

AXIOM OF
A SUCCESSFUL STRATEGY

A strategy of a company or firm is considered successful when a plethora of new products and services move from the emerging quadrant to the growth quadrant, allowing the company or firm's quadrant to be maintained or to change according to a strategic metric.

- The major task of the Managing Partner or CEO is to maintain or change the firm or company's position in its life cycle quadrant.

- The goal is to move your firm or company to a maturing quadrant and maintain that position. Unfortunately your markets are continually moving toward the aging quadrant, and a successful strategy will keep moving new products and services into the emerging quadrant allowing the firm or company to sustain its life cycle

AXIOM OF
LINE AND STAFF INVOLVEMENT

To be fully effective, formulation of strategy must be accomplished by line managers and partners with complete support from the staff managers and partners of the company or firm.

- Understanding line and staff accountability for the strategic plan is essential for its success
- Line VPs and key Partners, should take complete accountability for implementing strategic action plans

AXIOM OF
UNIT INTEGRATION:

For maximum effectiveness, individual department strategies must integrate with and support the corporate or firm strategy. Otherwise, these units will pursue their own objectives at the expense of the company or firm.

- A CEO or Managing Partner should never waste time developing strategy without complete implementation by the line departments of the organization

AXIOM OF
THE DRIVING FORCE(S):

When an organization takes the time and effort to identify the Driving Force(s) of its mission, and communicates this to the organization, a strategy for the Driving Force(s) increases the degree of success of that mission.

- Managers and Partners can take action at will without the need to focus on the uncritical many issues
- Direction of the organization as to products and services is
- determined by what is driving it to succeed

AXIOM OF
A CHANGING MARKET

Those CEOs and Managing Partners of companies and firms who continually monitor the product and service mix of its major competitors will be the first to notice a change in the market and the first to adapt their own products and services.

- An introduction of a competitive new product or service, not a line extension, is normally a sign of a change in the market not a change in the product.

AXIOM OF
CHANGING COMPANY QUADRANTS

Except for a startup entity, a company or firm can only change or maintain the quadrant in which it resides by redefining its Driving Force with Emerging Products and Services.

- Only a startup company or firm has no control over a driving force, and rides the emerging product or service regardless of what quadrant its market is in

- A company or firm finding itself in a Maturing or Aging position of the quadrant can only change its quadrant position by redefining its Driving Force

- The quadrant life cycle of a company or firm is the same as that of its products and services, and reflects heavily upon how innovative the organization is in developing new products and services which relate to the driving force

- When a company or firm moves from a mature quadrant to an aging quadrant, it reflects the aging products and services within its driving force, and when that driving force stops generating new emerging products and services then the company or firm must change its driving force to do so, or cease existence

AXIOM OF
COMPANY SUSTAINABILITY

Those companies who have a formal, annual process for continuing to develop emerging products and services as a part of their strategy will be most apt to remain or change position within their life cycle quadrant, and remain the market leader.

- In developing a CEO or Managing Partner's vision, defining the products and services within the prescribed markets is critical to remain a viable entity, and market leader

- Ongoing new products are required to be a formal part of the strategic plan, and doing so insures that the company remains in the quadrant it prefers

AXIOM OF
MARKETS AND PRODUCTS

The market for a company or firm's products and services is dynamic in nature, always changing with each second of time. A company or firm's products and services within each market are more static in nature, but with consistent adjustment required that parallels market change.

- Competitive tracking is key to proper strategy

AXIOM OF
THE STRATEGIC MARKET

A company or firm's market for its products and services should be in direct proportion to its available resources to compete with the competitive products and services within that market.

- It is better to be the biggest fish in a small pond, than being the smallest fish in a big pond. Small fish are easily eaten by larger fish

AXIOM OF
STRATEGIC MARKET EFFECTS

A strategy produces a series of effects on the market, with the first effect on the market immediate and observable, simultaneous with implementation of the strategic plan. The other effects on the market emerge subsequently and are unforeseen, normally caused by a competitive counter-initiative on a CEO or Managing Partner's strategy.

- A CEO or Managing Partner must always include the Axiom of Competitive Blocks within the strategy for the company or firm's products and services

AXIOM OF
OPTIMAL PRODUCT LIFE CYCLES

Normally, the optimal product and service life cycle is to have approximately 75% of your offerings in Mature & Aging quadrants, and 25% in Emerging & Growth quadrants.

- Strategy and strategic planning reflect the ability of the management team to consistently bring new products and services from Emerging and Growth quadrants to the Maturing quadrant

AXIOM OF
PRODUCT-SERVICE LIFE CYCLES

*A company or firm's products and services will have longer
life cycles and greater profitability when consistent adjustment
to market changes occur on a periodic basis.*

- Effective strategic planning demands annual analysis of the status of products and services
- Accountability for the life cycles of a company or firm's products and services is a line accountability

AXIOM OF
COMPETITIVE PRODUCTS AND SERVICES

*A company or firm's strategy is only as effective as its ability to
know the products and services of its major competitors in the
market in which it competes.*

- Business intelligence is as important about competitive products and services as it is for the products and services of the firm or company
- Normally a competitive new product or service is a sign of a market change, not a product change
- Tracking competitive products of a firm or company is also tracking the changes in the markets in which they compete

AXIOM OF
COMPETITIVE RESISTANCE

*Strategic Plans are not definite predictions. Their purpose is to
minimize or neutralize the competitive resistance impeding the
accomplishment of the firm or company's mission.*

- It is the combining of the Strategic Plan with the Operational plan that successful companies and firms undertake on an ongoing basis

AXIOM OF
COMPETITIVE BLOCKS

If the planned strategy of a company or firm is correct, but the CEO or Managing Partner does not include competitive blocks to anticipated counter-initiatives by key competitors, the unforeseen effects on the market will neutralize the strategy of the CEO or Managing Partner.

- A CEO or Managing Partner must always anticipate a competitive counter-initiative within the market that is a response to the CEO or Managing Partner's strategic action plans

AXIOM OF
COMPETITIVE BUSINESS MODELS

Those CEOs and Managing Partners of companies and firms who continually monitor the business model of competitive products and services will be the first to notice a change in the market over those who do not.

- By monitoring the business model of a competitive product or service, a company or firm will more likely acknowledge a change in the market for future products and services.

- A good example of this is that ARM Holdings, a UK company, is the leader in mobile device operating systems but does not manufacture any items themselves. It licenses the technology to those who do. However, monitoring ARM's product offerings identifies the roadmap for Apple, Samsung, and all other companies who manufacture mobile devices.

AXIOM OF
EXTENDING CURRENT MARKETS

Those companies or firms that have an ongoing strategy to extend their current markets will beat the markets and will automatically beat the competition.

- Stop trying to beat the competition…..start beating the market. Just like a golf match. The real contest is against the course, not your opponent. Beat the course, and you beat the opponent. Beat the market and you beat your competition

AXIOM OF
CHANGING DECISION FACTORS

Those companies or firms that utilize a strategy to use their current products and services to extend their current markets will be able to change the decision factors with competition within those extended markets, but not in the current markets.

- Having a strategy of becoming a big fish in a new small pond allows the big fish to influence the competitive marketing mix within that small pond and establish a short term advantage

AXIOM OF
NEW EMERGING MARKETS

New emerging markets will always emanate from a significant change in a Maturing Market's products and services which have emerged as a totally new offering to the marketplace.

- Emerging products and services that utilize price as the most important quality normally become commoditized in the Growth quadrant, since competitors with least cost capability will make it less profitable to market them

AXIOM OF
EMERGING PRODUCTS & SERVICES

Emerging products and services that utilize price as the sole quality of emergence will always have a short life cycle within a marketplace.

- Emerging products and services that utilize price as the most important quality normally become commoditized in the Growth quadrant, since competitors with least cost capabilities will make it less profitable to market them

AXIOM OF
THE LIFE CYCLE OF EMERGING PRODUCTS

Emerging products and services that emanate from a maturing market but do not develop or become a part of a totally new emerging market will move quickly back to the maturing quadrant from which it emanated.

- Emerging products and services that do not develop a new emerging market or act as a player within an emerging new market will have a short growth cycle, and move quickly back into the maturing market quadrant
- Emerging products and services that are driven from a maturing market have the tendency to increase short term sales unless they become a part of an emerging new market

AXIOM OF
AGING PRODUCTS & SERVICES

Aging products and services must have recurring replenishment of value or they become commoditized by competitive interaction with the client base.

- In order to maintain growth within the company or firm, the organization's aging products and services must continually receive a shot of adrenalin to remain viable

AXIOM OF
DECISIVE TIMING

Those companies and firms that implement a strategy to use their current products and services to extend their current markets have a very short time span to implement the decision factors with competition.

- A strategy of becoming a big fish in a new small pond allows the big fish to influence the competitive marketing mix within that small pond, but other larger fish will enter that segment of the pond unless the company moves quickly to set up the decision factors for the small pond

AXIOM OF
STRATEGIC MANAGEMENT DEPTH

Those companies and firms that implement a strategy to use their current products and services to extend their current markets but do not have management depth to control the growth of the extended market will lose to competitors who have management depth.

- Normally this is when a company or firm will violate the Axiom of the Strategic Market, above

AXIOM OF
A FULFILLED STRATEGY

Fulfillment of a CEO or Managing Partner's strategy always occurs much slower than what is planned, and then when fulfillment becomes obvious the operations move immediately faster than what is planned.

- This axiom underscores the importance of having a formal strategic plan linked to formal operational plans, so that when the strategy becomes fulfilled the function of control (metrics) will allow leadership management at all levels of the organization

- When a strategy is fulfilled, the operational plans become obsolete unless they are continually updated to address the fulfillment within the products and markets of the firm or company

AXIOM OF
EXCESSIVE SWAGGER

Whenever a company or firm becomes overly convinced of one's invulnerability to the marketplace, a competitor will enter and take your market position.

- A manager or partner should always realize that it is the marketplace that your company or firm is fighting, and if one recognizes that the markets are continually changing at a snail's pace beneath our feet, the successful companies and firms will continually adjust their products and services to remain successful

AXIOM'S IN MANAGEMENT TENETS:

PLANNING

Planning

To formulate a scheme or program for the accomplishment or attainment of a manager or partner's objectives, or the mission of the organization.

Planning is an area which most managers prefer the most. It is also an area where the direct reports of a partner or manager differ on how well they plan. When direct reports are included in the planning process, the manager or partner is viewed as a manager-delegator and commitment by the direct reports normally occurs.

The following Axioms in Management Tenets are used by successful CEOs and Managing Partners in implementing their planning of operations.

AXIOM OF
SUCCESSFUL PLANNING:

Those managers and partners who solicit employee input into their planning process will normally accomplish more objectives than those who do not by a factor of 8.

- Since managers and partners get paid to achieve objectives, including those subordinates who will do the work of the plan increases odds on success

AXIOM OF
PLANNING SUPERIORITY

Those organizations that plan their tactics and objectives in a formalized (written) manner, and control the accomplishment of their mission, are consistently superior to their competition.

- Written plans always dictate success.

AXIOM OF
FORMAL OBJECTIVES AND METRICS:

Those companies who manage their business operationally with formal objectives and metrics are always more successful in accomplishing the mission than those companies who do not use formal objectives and metrics.

- It is the metric that is the most critical for successful CEOs and Managing Partners, and when the metric is formally written out for all to see, there is a team dynamic which insulates the organization from failure

AXIOMS IN MANAGEMENT TENETS:
ACTION PLANS

AXIOM OF
WASTED RESOURCES

When decisions affecting the key objectives of the organization are made without formalized (written) Action Plans, the resources of time and money are normally wasted.

- Formal Action Plans drive accountability by a manager or partner
- Metrics determine the accomplishment of the plan

AXIOM OF
ADEQUATE FOLLOW-UP

Formal Action Plans to resolve problems are only as effective as the quality and quantity of management follow-up which occurs on an ongoing basis.

- Without accountable follow-up by a manager or partner, Action Plans seldom are accomplished

AXIOM OF
ACTION PLAN UTILIZATION

Formal Action Plans should not be utilized unless there is a need to establish accountability between divisions, departments, or individuals performing a task or project.

- Beware: Overuse of Action Plans = a paper mill!

AXIOM OF
NON-COMMITMENT

When there is a need for formal Action Plans, managers and partners achieve limited results when the plans are developed exclusively by the managers or partners having authority to dictate the objective and metrics.

- Direct report input is key to their commitment to the plan itself.

AXIOM OF
ACCEPTING ACCOUNTABILITY

Managers and partners achieve maximum results from using formalized Action Plans only when every person involved in the Action Plan is present during its development, and accepts accountability, not responsibility.

- Direct report input is key, as above.

AXIOM OF
REPETITIOUS WORK

Managers who develop formalized Action Plans without metrics will achieve limited results, and require employees to repeat the work several times.

- Metrics offer the manager and partner the control required for achieving success in planning
- Look for comments, "…must be flexible around here" as it reflects on the manager or partner

AXIOM OF
MANAGEMENT WORK

The more accountability a person accepts within a company or firm, and particularly during the development of Action Plans, the more management work is required and less specialist work.

- Action Plans require the team or department members to accept accountability for accomplishing various parts of the plan.

"It is better to be a big fish in a small pond, than a small fish in a big pond. Big fish eat small fish."

Greg Weismantel

AXIOMS IN MANAGEMENT TENETS:
ORGANIZING

Organizing

Is a function of leadership management. Organizing is to arrange the work of an organization in a coherent, orderly, and structured pattern, so that it can be accomplished in the most productive manner in achieving the objective or the mission of the organization.

A manager or a partner of a company or firm should reorganize his unit of work every year in order to maintain a high degree of efficiency within the unit as well as to analyze and update its core processes.

The following Axioms in Management Tenets are used by successful CEOs and Managing Partners in structuring your organization for efficiency.

AXIOM OF
SUCCESSFUL RESTRUCTURING:

Successful organizing or restructuring a company or firm only occurs when a manager or partner organizes the department, or the team, <u>around the work</u> required to achieve the mission or objective, <u>not around the personnel</u> you have to do the work.

- Consistent problems will occur within the organization when an individual is chosen by a manager or partner who does not have the skill set to accomplish the job but has the best personality to "fit in" with the organization

AXIOM OF
RESTRUCTURING OBJECTIVES

In restructuring an organization, managers and partners should recognize that when the business is good the objective is "not to lose one person," whereas when business is bad the objective is to "reduce head count to breakeven or profitability."

- The rule of thumb is that each year the management should restructure for efficiency and productivity gains
- 98% of the time the objective is "not to lose one person"

AXIOM OF EMPLOYEE NET WORTH

Every employee of the company or firm, regardless of whether they are partner or executive, provides a financial net worth to the organization based upon the subjective number of dollars of revenue for which they are responsible, divided by the total salary, bonus and benefit of the individual.

- Determining the net worth of each employee is an important exercise for a CEO or Managing Partner when restructuring the organization on an annual basis

AXIOM OF
MANAGEMENT DEPTH

The most successful companies and firms always have an ongoing process of developing managers and partners from within, thereby providing an overwhelming depth of managerial talent at all levels of a company or firm's structure.

- Successful CEOs and Managing Partners have the accountability of insuring management depth at all levels of the organization

AXIOMS IN MANAGEMENT TENETS:
DELEGATION

AXIOM OF
SPECIFIC RESULTS

In delegation subordinates must know clearly what specific results they are expected to produce, and must agree to accept it.

- The metrics of control are as critical to the manager or partner as they are to the subordinate receiving them

AXIOM OF
ABILITY TO ACCOMPLISH

Managers and partners must know the skills, abilities, and motivations of the subordinate before delegating the work, so that subordinates are capable of accomplishing the given task.

- Otherwise the work returns to your desk

AXIOM OF
IDENTIFIED METRICS

Managers and partners must help their subordinates understand the requirements and metrics of completing the work, and subordinates must agree with the metrics set.

- What choices do you have when metrics are not agreed-to by the subordinate to whom you are delegating the work? You either find someone else to delegate to, or do it yourself

AXIOM OF
ADEQUATE AUTHORITY

In delegating a particular responsibility to a subordinate, managers and partners must also delegate sufficient authority to make the necessary decisions to achieve the expected results.

- Otherwise the work returns to your desk

AXIOM OF
MANAGEMENT HELP

Managers and partners must make themselves available when help is required by a subordinate to complete the work and accomplish the objective.

- Following the delegation of the work and metrics to a subordinate, the manager or partner takes on a staff responsibility to support and serve the subordinate

AXIOM OF
SUCCESSFUL INTERVIEWING:

Successful Interviewing involves the evaluation of a person's _skill sets_ that they bring to the job, along with the appraisal of the _chemistry_ they must have to fit into the organization's culture, so that it can be determined that a person should or should not fill an available position in the company.

- Evaluation by the manager or partner of the individual's skill set for the position is objective, yes or no

- Appraisal by the manager or partner of the chemistry to fit into the organization's culture is subjective. This is the most important of the two requirements, and the most difficult

AXIOM OF INTERVIEWING
ACCOUNTABILITY

The responsibility for interviewing can be delegated; the accountability for selecting people cannot be delegated from the manager or partner with authority to make the selection decision.

- A CEO or Managing Partner of a company or firm, or a Manager or Partner of a department in that company or firm, should never complain about the personnel of his or her entire organization because it is they who are accountable for the selection of the people who have the responsibility for achieving the objectives of the mission.

AXIOM OF
LACK OF MANAGEMENT DEPTH

The lack of management depth within an organization is directly proportional to the amount of participation by the manager or partner in properly selecting individuals for employment with the company or firm.

- Too often a manager or partner delegates the responsibility and authority for selecting people to those individuals who are not skilled in the interviewing techniques of hiring for skill set and culture of the company or firm.

"An army of lions commanded by a deer will never be an army of lions."

Napoleon Bonaparte

FUNCTION OF LEADERSHIP-MANAGEMENT: LEADING

AXIOMS IN MANAGEMENT TENETS:
LEADING OR LEADERSHIP

Leading or Leadership

Is one of the Six Functions of Management, and is defined as showing the way or guiding your direct reports by going in advance of others. It is characterized by achieving objectives with metrics through a team effort, through and with others.

One cannot train a manager or partner to lead others, it is a natural phenomenon of accountability, and it is a criterion for being a solid manager or partner that you automatically lead in advance of others, and you are the first to stand when asked for a volunteer.

AXIOMS IN MANAGEMENT TENETS:
ACCOUNTABILITY

AXIOM OF
RESPONSIBILITY

Responsibility implies the trustworthy performance of fixed duties or work, and it implies that a specific person is designated to accomplish that work.

- Note that responsibility does not include any authority provided by a higher authority to make key decisions

AXIOM OF
ACCOUNTABILITY

Accountability is the combining of the responsibility, the fixed duties or work, along with the <u>authority</u> given by a higher level to complete the work, and <u>agreed-to</u> by the individual accepting the responsibility.

- Accountability does include authority with the work, but also includes agreement by the subordinate

AXIOM OF
MAXIMIZING ACHIEVEMENT

Those managers and partners who drill down full authority to make decisions for their responsibilities to their direct reports will achieve more objectives than doer-managers who drill down partial authority to their direct reports.

- Keep in mind, whenever a manager or partner delegates work and authority to complete the work to any level of the organization, it must always be accompanied by the function of Control in the form of metrics

AXIOMS IN MANAGEMENT TENETS:
DECISION MAKING
AXIOM OF
THE REAL VS. THE APPARENT PROBLEM

After identifying the "apparent problem," when a manager or partner does not gather more facts, the "real problem" is usually not considered.

- What happens when the real problem is not considered? The team begins work on the apparent problem, which is the symptom to the real problem
- The manager or partner is accountable to insure that the real problem is addressed

AXIOM OF
WASTED EFFORT

When a manager or partner does not identify the real problem, the subordinates usually work toward achieving the wrong objective, and wasted effort occurs.

- For what do Managers get paid? Achieving Objectives

AXIOM OF
PROPER OBJECTIVES AND TACTICS

When the proper objective is identified, the proper work will automatically follow. (The corollary is also true)

- The proper objective emanates from the real problem

AXIOM OF
THE 20/80 RULE

In any number of occurrences of an event, approximately 20% account for 80% of the results accomplished. (Pareto's Constant – Wilfredo Pareto, 1848-1923)

- This axiom is utilized in most management tenets

AXIOMS IN MANAGEMENT
TENETS: **COMMUNICATIONS**

AXIOM OF
UNDERSTANDING THE OBJECTIVE(S):

Managers and partners who have a thorough understanding of the objectives and metrics of performance for their unit or department communicate better with their subordinates than those who do not.

- Utilizing a common vocabulary of terms improves communication of the objective and metric
- Including subordinates in your planning process, and metric setting process is the key ingredient for proper communication

AXIOM OF
EMOTION IN COMMUNICATING:

Managers and partners who utilize emotion in their communication techniques receive a higher degree of feedback of their message.

- Emotion in communication is an important method in gaining and holding attention. One easy method is in lowering then raising your voice when speaking to individuals, or vice versa

AXIOMS IN MANAGEMENT TENETS:
LEADERSHIP SKILLS

AXIOM OF RECOGNIZED ACCOMPLISHMENT

Managers and partners tend to accomplish results according to metric when they are recognized for their accomplishment.

- Recognition does not infer a monetary requirement

AXIOM OF MONEY AS A MOTIVATOR

Motivation to accomplish results has a short time span when money is utilized as a motivating factor.

- Money has a very short time span in motivating individuals. What have you done for me lately?

AXIOM OF INNOVATION IN MANAGEMENT:

Those managers and partners who motivate and encourage their subordinates to innovate on the job, have more satisfied employees and workers within their unit.

- Innovation requires empowerment and driving the authority to innovate down to lower levels
- Whenever a manager or partner drives authority to lower levels, metrics are your safety belt.

AXIOM OF
PRODUCTIVE MEETINGS

Productive meetings can only occur within a company or firm if there is a manager, partner or team leader present who has the authority to make a decision and take action on the results of that meeting's objective.

- Meetings without a participant having the authority to make a decision and take action should not be held

AXIOM OF
TRAINING & DEVELOPMENT

Training is 90% driven by the company or firm and 10% by the individual; while Development is 90% driven by the individual and 10% by the company or firm.

- A CEO or Managing Partner must recognize that providing the tools and techniques of leadership is training, and that it is up to the individual to utilize the tools to develop themselves

AXIOM OF
DEVELOPING LEADER MANAGERS

Those CEOs, Managing Partners and other managers of a company or firm who place specific objectives and metrics for developing leader managers in-house, and evaluate and appraise their direct reports annually if these are accomplished, will have ongoing lines of management depth within their companies and firms.

- This axiom is at the heart of developing leader-managers and not just leaders. If a manager at any level of the organization does not accomplish this objective it should affect his annual salary increase or bonus

FUNCTION OF LEADERSHIP-MANAGEMENT: TEAMWORK

AXIOMS IN MANAGEMENT TENETS
TEAMWORK

Teamwork

To take harmonious action in a unified or "team" effort for obtaining active help, cooperation, understanding, and agreement from another person, department or segment of the business, over which there is no authority.

Teamwork is important because rarely can a partner, manager, department or organization achieve its mission by itself. It requires the harmonious help and coordination of other people in other teams. However, even perfect teamwork and coordination will not guarantee success unless the line of authority is clearly defined for solid decision making.

AXIOM OF
LINE & STAFF TEAMWORK

Key Objectives are best accomplished when Line managers or partners accountable for the key objectives of the company or firm, receive full support from the Staff managers or partners who are accountable for supporting the line, and Line does not have to perform Staff responsibilities.

- When staff does not support the line, the accountability for achieving the objective remains with line, and line must perform the staff work for the objectives.
- History Lesson: in the '80s, IT departments (staff) with mainframes did not support sales and marketing (line), and so sales and marketing units brought PCs into the workforce and spreadsheets proliferated

AXIOM OF
LINE INDEPENDENCE

Whenever Line managers and partners <u>do not receive full support and service</u> from Staff units, the Line managers and partners will perform this function themselves.

- Understanding the roles of line and staff is critical for accomplishing the mission.

AXIOM OF
STAFF ACCEPTANCE

Staff support and service will be accepted and utilized by Line areas <u>if and only if</u> the support and service is appropriate and exactly as the Line unit requires to achieve the objective.

- When staff provides the proper support and line refuses it, staff will not support the line thereafter

AXIOM OF
STAFF REFUSAL

If Staff units refuse to provide the exact support that Line managers and partners require, <u>whether requested or not</u>, the Line unit will perform the function itself, AND REFUSE TO USE STAFF IN THE FUTURE.

- Marketing departments are quite often staff units, but if they do not support the line units of the company or firm, line units will do the work alone

AXIOM OF
LINE TO STAFF TRANSITION

Line managers or partners who drill-down objectives with metrics to lower levels with the authority required to accomplish those objective, transition to become staff managers to the very people to whom you have drilled-down the objectives.

- The CEO or Managing Partner is the top line manager in the organization. Whenever a CEO or Managing Partner drills down an objective to a Vice President or other Partner, that CEO or Managing Partner becomes staff to the VP or Partner, requiring full support and service in helping the VP or Partner to achieve the objectives.

AXIOM OF
COMMUNICATION REQUIREMENTS

The amount of Teamwork required to achieve the objective or mission of the firm or company depends upon the <u>requirements of communication</u> by the diverse organizations or departments and the degree of interdependence of these units.

- The amount of communication required by a team is in proportion to the amount of teamwork and coordination required by the team.

AXIOM OF
CONFLICT RESOLUTION

Managers and partners who establish accountabilities with metrics between team members and team leaders automatically eliminate over 90% of all team conflicts, and help resolve the other 10% before they fester into major issues.

- The two most important management tenets that a manager or partner must master to become most professional are metrics and accountability

AXIOM OF
THE OPEN DOOR POLICY

Managers and partners who do not have actual accountability for a key objective of the organization, <u>and who have no direct line authority over those managers and partners who are accountable</u>, have the duty and obligation to report to higher levels of management whenever there is a severe risk in the accomplishment of a key objective, and when no action is taken by the accountable manager or partner.

FUNCTION OF LEADERSHIP-MANAGEMENT: CONTROL

AXIOMS IN MANAGEMENT TENETS:
CONTROL

Control

A metric of comparison for measuring or verifying the results of an objective or unit of work.

A manager or partner utilizes the function of control so that there are guidelines or parameters that allow their subordinates to take action without having the manager or partner do so.

The two most important tenets that a CEO or Managing Partner should master are accountability and metrics, because both express leadership and control requirements for success.

AXIOM OF
THE QUANTIFIABLE VS. QUALITATIVE METRICS

Managers and partners achieve more objectives through and with their team when measurement Metrics are quantifiable with Key Performance Indicators (KPI) than when they are qualitative with yes or no measurements or metrics based upon time achieved.

- Control is best implemented by managers and partners when subordinates have a quantifiable metric that is a numerical part of their specialist work

AXIOM OF
THE REALISTIC METRIC

Managers and partners achieve more objectives through and with their team or department when measurement metrics are realistic to those performing the work.

- Whenever metrics are unrealistic or too difficult or too easy to achieve, the team morale is impacted and there is little team or department motivation to achieve the objective.

AXIOM OF
TOLERABLE LIMITS

Managers and partners can control by exception by first establishing metrics of performance for objectives, and then setting tolerable limits within which the subordinates can work without consulting the manager.

- Tolerable limits are also called parameters, and managers and partners should establish these so that authority can be provided to subordinates to make decisions and take action within those tolerable limits

AXIOM OF
INSPECTION OF QUALITY

Managers and partners achieve more objectives through and with their team when measurement metrics and authority to take action are known by the workers performing the work and performing the inspection of the work, so that when deviations occur they have the proper amount of authority to take action without their manager or partner being present.

- There is no difference between authority in this axiom and the authority required for proper delegation.

AXIOM OF
SELF-EVALUATION

Whenever an individual evaluates their own performance, there is a greater tendency to be more demanding on themselves regarding accomplishment of the objective and the tactics used.

- I have asked managers and partners hundreds of times if this axiom is valid, and have never had one person say that it is not. My next question is, "…since we agree this is true, then why don't you allow your people to evaluate themselves?"

AXIOM OF
TEAM APPRAISAL

Whenever individuals evaluate themselves as a team in self-evaluation, the manner in which their task was performed by that team should be acknowledged by the person to whom the team is accountable.

- Evaluation is objective in nature, and should be accomplished by the individuals
- Appraisal is subjective in nature, and should be accomplished by the manager, partner, or team leader (manager)

" True leaders don't create followers, they create more leaders."

J.Sakiya Sandifer.

"The dictionary is the only place where success comes before work."

Vince Lombardi

Vocabulary & Axioms for Professional Managers and Partners
2nd Edition © Gregory N. Weismantel, 2014

About the Author

After having spent several years in senior and general management positions with major companies, Greg Weismantel has been involved in Management Consulting and Leadership Management Developmint for over 25 years.

Greg spent 14 years in Executive Sales/Marketing and Brand Management positions with Kraft-General Foods, three years as President/CEO of Manor House Foods, three years as Vice President for Professional Marketers Inc. and two years as President of Aquitec, Inc. of Chicago. His Management Consulting experience began as a Senior VP for Louis Allen Associates, a top 100 management consulting firm located in Palo Alto, CA, where he specialized in strategic planning and organizational restructuring.

In 1992, Weismantel founded the Epic Management Group, and developed an "Effective Management Process" linked with "Leadership Management" and implemented these throughout the United States for Asea Brown Boveri, Atlanta GA (ABB USA).

He has performed strategic planning and leadership management initiatives with Flakt, Inc., Asea Brown Boveri US, Arthur Andersen, Commonwealth Edison, Diamond Walnut, Martin-Marietta, Lockheed, Zebra Technology, Johnson Industries, Doran Scales, Norix Group, Mueller LLC and other companies and firms.

Mr. Weismantel is a graduate of the University of Notre Dame, and holds an MBA from Loyola University of Chicago. He has been recognized by his peers and listed in _Who's Who in America_ each year since 1993. In addition he is Army Strong, having served as an Officer in the 2nd Squadron - 14th Armored Cavalry, and reached the rank of Captain.

"The most successful leadership managers that I have witnessed at companies and firms are those who have developed someone to eventually be their boss."

Greg Weismantel